Off-Balance Sheet Activities

OFF-BALANCE SHEET ACTIVITIES

Edited by

Joshua Ronen, Anthony Saunders, and Ashwinpaul C. Sondhi

Published under the auspices of The Vincent C. Ross
Institute of Accounting Research

The Leonard N. Stern School of Business,
New York University

and

New York University Salomon Center

QUORUM BOOKS

New York • Westport, Connecticut • London

Library of Congress Cataloging-in-Publication Data

Off-balance sheet activities / Joshua Ronen, Anthony Saunders, and
  Ashwinpaul C. Sondhi, editors.
     p. cm.
     "Published under the auspices of the Vincent C. Ross Institute of
  Accounting Research, the Leonard N. Stern School of Business, New
  York University, and New York University Salomon Center."
     Includes index.
     ISBN 0–89930–613–6 (lib. bdg. : alk. paper)
     1. Banks and banking—United States—Accounting. 2. Financial
  institutions—United States—Accounting. 3. Financial statements.
  4. Disclosure in accounting. I. Ronen, Joshua. II. Saunders, Anthony.
  III. Sondhi, Ashwinpaul C. IV. Vincent C. Ross Institute of
  Accounting Research. V. New York University Salomon Center.
  HG1708.044   1990
  657'.833303—dc20   90–8909

British Library Cataloguing in Publication Data is available.

Library of Congress Catalog Card Number: 90-8909
ISBN: 0-89930-613-6

First published in 1990

Quorum Books, 88 Post Road West, Westport, CT 06881
An imprint of Greenwood Publishing Group, Inc.

Printed in the United States of America

The paper used in this book complies with the
Permanent Paper Standard issued by the National
Information Standards Organization (Z39.48-1984).

10 9 8 7 6 5 4 3 2 1

Contents

Preface

This book had its origins in a New York University Conference jointly undertaken by the Vincent C. Ross Institute of Accounting Research and the Salomon Brothers Center for the Study of Financial Institutions at the Stern School of Business. It brought together accounting and finance academic researchers, along with practitioners and regulators, with the objective of gaining insights into and proposing meaningful solutions to those issues raised by the current proliferation of off-balance sheet transactions. Those transactions are analyzed in terms of risk and valuation, appropriate regulation, and accounting standards.

Successful conferences generate proceedings that call for wider dissemination. In this case, the proceedings have been published in the *Journal of Accounting, Auditing and Finance*, volume 4, number 2, 1989. In order to reach the student of finance, the practitioners and regulators in financial institutions and markets, as well as to update the proceedings, we have prepared this hard cover edition of *Off-Balance Sheet Activities*.

We believe that the insights and solutions offered in this volume are sounder as well as fuller than could have been reached by the two disciplines working separately. In short, the interdisciplinary activity, always difficult to arrange and to manage, has justified itself.

Indeed, we plan a biannual series of these conferences with commissioned papers concentrating on off-balance sheet activities of savings banks, and then investment banks to follow the commercial bank applications. It would be useful to hold a final conference on the role of off-balance sheet aspects of the activities of international financial institutions.

Part I

Off–Balance Sheet Activities and Banking

ANTHONY SAUNDERS*

One of the most important strategic developments in recent years has been the move by banks into new areas of off-balance sheet (OBS) banking. This has been a natural outcome of (i) the increased competition (narrowing of margins) for traditional banking products, such as commercial loans, (ii) the rapid growth and diffusion of new technologies such as CHIPS, SWIFT, etc., and (iii) new financial market innovations, such as futures, options, and swaps. While this trend has been evident for some years, regulators have only recently started to collect information and monitor the growth in exposure of the banks involved and to put in place regulatory proposals to control the growth and risk of such off-balance sheet activities.

OBS banking may be broadly divided into six different categories of activity: (1) loan commitments, (2) future and forward contracts, (3) standby contracts/letters of credit, (4) options arrangements, (5) swaps, and (6) loan sales (securitization).

The notional exposure of U.S. banks in these areas is reported quarterly in Schedule L of the Federal Reserves Reports of Condition. Thus, for example, the 14,111 Schedule L reporting banks in December 1986 showed total balance sheet assets of $2,923 billion compared to off-balance sheet items of $2,488 billion or 85 percent of assets. The largest items were: commitments to purchase foreign currencies ($892.6 billion), loan commitments ($570.8 billion), interest rate swaps ($367 billion) and standby letters to U.S. addresses ($131 billion).

However, aggregate figures tend to mask the much higher relative exposures of the large money-center banks. For example, Citibank's off-balance sheet activities are currently over four times

---

*Professor of Finance, New York University.

larger than its on-balance sheet activities. In recognition of the growth of such activities the Federal Reserve is phasing in the implementation of risk-based capital standards that become fully effective (along with the other countries of the Organization for Economic Cooperation and Development [OECD]) at the end of 1992. The essential concept of risk-based capital is that OBS activities expose banks to a variety of risks and that capital adequacy can only be judged in the context of such risks. Appendix I shows the Federal Reserve's final risk-based capital scheme (January 1989). As might be noted this capital adequacy scheme monitors just the default or credit risk of these activities with an assessment as to the interest rate risk of these activities to follow in the future.

In this environment, the three papers on banking and OBS activities are indeed timely. In the first paper ''Off-Balance Sheet Activities and the Underinvestment Problem in Banking'', James shows how loan sales with recourse and stand-by letter of credit (SLC)-backed loans allow the bank to specialize in bearing credit risk while the purchaser of the loan (or SLC beneficiary) ''funds'' the loan. As a result, by separating the funding of the loan from credit guarantee services a bank can earn fee income without expanding its balance sheet. Moreover, he also shows that the cash-flow payoffs, from loan sales with recourse, exhibit very similar characteristics to secured debt and thus are very attractive to both investors and bankers. In particular, the separation of funding from credit guarantees allows banks, indirectly, to finance more projects than in a world without loan sales or SLCs; or in the parlance of corporate finance, it allows banks to mitigate the tendency towards underinvestment in the real sector when projects are debt financed. From a policy perspective James's paper is additionally instructive since it shows that the imposition of traditional capital asset ratio requirements and fixed priced deposit insurance actually encourage the growth of OBS activities. This suggests that any imposition of risk-based capital or risk-based deposit insurance premia may actually increase the degree of underinvestment in potentially profitable projects. Hence there appears to be an inherent trade-off between risk-based capital (or risk-based deposit insurance) and the scale of underinvestment thought desirable.

In the second paper, ''Are Loan Sales Really Off-Balance Sheet?'', Gorton and Pennacchi assess whether loan sales carry an implicit (if not explicit) guarantee that the purchaser has the option to put (sell) the loan back to the bank sometime prior to maturity. While regulators require loan sales to be without recourse, in order for the bank to save on capital and reserve requirements, such activities appear to destroy the valuable specialized function of bankers as loan/credit monitors. If loan sales do carry such a sell-back guarantee or option feature then the purchasing investor would be concerned about the default risk of the bank that sold the loan. Moreover, this guarantee feature appears to be very similar to the SLC guarantees that banks issue to back commercial paper issues. Using a unique data base, Gorton and Pennacchi appear to find that there is a bank-specific risk premium impounded into loan sale interest rates although this premium might be less than that on commercial paper. They suggest two reasons as to why investors may be more concerned about a bank defaulting on its guarantees in the commercial paper case. First, since these guarantees are default vulnerable, the SLC guarantee on commercial paper can only be exercised at the time of commercial paper maturity whereas the implicit guarantee of resale of a loan back to the bank is an option that can be exercised at any time (i.e., it is more valuable). Second, banks do a more efficient job of monitoring borrowers whose loans they sell compared to borrowers who issue commercial paper.

While the first two papers are concerned with micro-economic issues related to banks' OBS activities, the third paper is concerned with macro– or monetary policy implications. In their paper "Money Demand and Off-Balance Sheet Liquidity: Empirical Analysis and Implications for Monetary Policy", Glick and Plaut argue that loan commitments and other off-balance sheet contingent liabilities provide a direct substitute for on-balance sheet money. That is, access to off-balance credit can augment and complement a firm's (or consumer's) access to liquidity and can alleviate conventional liquidity shortages. Using macro-economic data, the authors estimate a traditional money demand function for the United States, supplemented by measures of unused loan commitments over the 1974–1987 period. Their most important finding suggests that unused loan commitments and traditional money items (cash and deposits) are negatively related (i.e., substitutes). That is, a high level of unused loan commitments can lower, ceteris paribus, the demand for money. This effect has important policy implications since the presence of loan commitments appear to weaken the relationship *between money, interest rates, and other macro-variables in the economy. This, in turn, suggests that policy makers may wish to either target, or at least closely track, a total liquidity variable which includes off-balance sheet credit lines rather than more narrow and traditional definitions of the money supply.*

Off–Balance Sheet Activities and the Underinvestment Problem in Banking

CHRISTOPHER JAMES*

This paper examines the incentives banks have to engage in "off–balance sheet" activities such as commercial loan sales and the issuance of standby letters of credit (SLCs). It shows that loan sales and loans backed by SLCs have payoff characteristics similar to secured debt. Like secured debt, these off–balance sheet activities permit banks to sell a portion of the cash flows associated with new investment opportunities. The ability to engage in off-balance sheet activities is shown to permit banks to invest in loans with positive net present values that they would pass up if restricted to deposit financing.

1. Introduction

There has been a dramatic growth over the past decade in what is called "off–balance sheet" banking. Examples include the issuance of standby letters of credit (SLCs) and commercial loan sales. An SLC is a bank-issued commitment to pay one party (called the beneficiary) in the event that the bank's customer (called the account party) fails to repay a loan or defaults on some other contractual obligation. In the event of default, the bank advances funds to the beneficiary in the amount of beneficiary's loss. Commercial loan sales involve the sale of newly originated bank loans to a third party (usually another bank). Loan sales are structured contractually so that the selling bank continues to service the loan even though title to the loan is transferred to the purchaser.

Loan sales and SLCs share two common features. First, they involve the separation of many of the services associated with bank lending, such as credit risk evaluation and loan servicing from the funding of a loan. For example, in a loan sale with recourse or in an SLC-backed loan the bank underwrites the credit risk and may service the loan, but the purchaser or beneficiary funds the loan. By separating the funding of a loan from these other activities, a bank can earn fee income without putting an asset or

---

*University of Oregon.

corresponding liability on its balance sheet. Second, as I show, loan sales and SLC-backed loans have payoff characteristics similar to collateralized or secured debt.

In this paper I examine the economic rationale for SLC issues and commercial loan sales. I show that like secured debt issues, loan sales and SLC issues permit banks to sell a portion of the cash flows associated with new loans or investment opportunities. By enabling banks to sell a portion of the cash flows associated with new investments, loan sales and SLCs provide a vehicle, similar to secured debt, through which banks can avoid the underinvestment problem that arises when a firm has risky debt outstanding. By an underinvestment problem I mean the tendency for firms with debt outstanding to pass up new positive net present value investments. This problem, described in detail in Myers (1977), arises when new investment opportunities reduce the risk of outstanding debt claims and effect a wealth transfer from stockholders to debt holders.

Although the payoff characteristics of loan sales and SLC-backed loans are similar to secured or collateralized debt, banks are generally prohibited from issuing collateralized deposits. Loan sales and SLCs therefore serve as one available substitute.[1] The hypothesis that loan sales and SLCs serve as substitutes for collateralized debt is referred to as the collateralization hypothesis.

The model of loan sales and SLC issues is used to analyze the effect of capital requirements and deposit insurance on the incentives banks have to engage in off–balance sheet activities. In particular, I show that capital requirements and fixed-rate deposit insurance exacerbate the underinvestment problem and increase the incentives to sell loans or issue SLCs. Capital requirements, which limit bank leverage, exacerbate the underinvestment problem by restricting a bank's ability to offset reductions in asset risk with increases in financial leverage. Fixed-rate deposit insurance can increase the underinvestment problem because with insurance the rate paid on a portion of the bank's liabilities will not adjust to reflect the marginal contribution of a new investment to the risk of a bank's assets.

The collateralization hypothesis yields several testable implications. First, the underinvestment problem will not be serious when a bank's deposits are not very risky. Therefore, the frequency of loan sales and SLCs is expected to increase with the risk of bank assets and with financial leverage. Second, the underinvestment problem is not likely to be serious for high-NPV (Net Present Value) or high-risk loans. Thus, loan sales and

---

1. Under federal law and regulation (12 USC 90 and 12 CRF 7.7410), national banks may pledge assets against public but not private deposits (see Hayes [1987]).

SLCs are likely to be used for low-risk loans to customers with a small amount of bank-specific capital (e.g., loans to investment grade borrowers). Finally, because the underinvestment problem is exacerbated by binding capital requirements, banks with equity capital at or below the legal limit are expected to use SLCs and loan sales more frequently. The institutional arrangements concerning loan sales and SLC issues as well as the results of previous empirical studies are consistent with the predictions of my model.

The paper is organized as follows. Section 2 provides a brief description of the loan sales and SLC markets and the current regulatory treatment of these activities. Section 3 presents the model. Section 4 discusses the empirical implications of the model. The final section summarizes and concludes.

2. Background

2.1. The Market for Commercial Loan Sales and SLCs

Commercial loan sales involve the sale of newly originated commercial loans. In most commercial loan sales, the selling bank continues to be responsible for servicing the loan, enforcing covenants, monitoring the financial condition of the borrower, and handling workouts and other problems that might arise in the event of default.[2] In exchange for providing these services the selling bank is compensated through a ''spread.'' The spread represents the difference between the rate paid by the borrower to the bank and the return promised to the purchaser of the loan.[3] Current bank regulations require that loans sold with recourse be treated as assets when calculating capital requirements. Moreover, the proceeds of loans sold with recourse are subject to reserve requirements.[4] As a result, commercial loans rarely are sold with recourse.[5]

---

2. As Gorton and Haubrich (1987) explain, loan sales typically are structured contractually as participations. A participation involves the creation of a new contract between the bank and the purchaser of the loan. The purchaser's contract is with the originating bank and not with the bank's customer.

3. The June 1, 1987 Senior Loan Officer Survey conducted by the Federal Reserve Board reports an average spread of fifteen basis points on commercial loan sales.

4. See Melvin (1986) for a description of the regulatory treatment of loan sales. If a depository institution sells a loan and agrees to be responsible for 75 percent or less of the losses from the loan, then under present regulations the proceeds from the sale are not reservable.

5. Loans sold without recourse raise concerns with the purchaser regarding the quality of loans sold (an adverse selection problem) and the diligence with which the selling bank will monitor the borrower after a sale (a moral hazard problem) (see Pennacchi [1987]). One technique used to provide the purchaser a credible assurance of the quality is for the selling bank to maintain or fund a portion of the loan sold. In addition, because most commercial loans sold are short-term and the selling bank

Information on the volume of commercial loans sold indicates a dramatic increase in sales over the past few years. For example, information from the Call Report indicates that the volume of loan sales increased from $23 billion in 1983 to $111 billion in 1986. Moreover, loan sales have grown relative to total commercial loans originated by commercial banks: from 7 percent of C&I (Commercial and Industrial) loans in 1983 to 25 percent of C&I loans in 1986.[6]

An SLC is a guarantee by a bank to pay the beneficiary if the bank's customer fails to repay a loan or perform some other contractual obligation. (For a description of the SLC market see Bennett [1986] or Koppenhaver [1987].) The majority of SLCs are used to back financial contracts such as commercial paper, municipal bonds, and direct loans. The issuer of an SLC agrees to advance funds to make the beneficiary whole in the event the account party defaults on the loan. The beneficiary of an SLC-backed loan therefore receives the right to the contracted payments associated with the loan and, in the event of default, receives a claim on the bank's assets equal to the losses guaranteed by the SLC.

Like the commercial loan sales market, the volume of SLCs has grown rapidly in recent years. For example, since 1980, SLCs outstanding have grown at an annual rate of 20 percent, from $47 billion to $169 billion in 1986. Moreover, SLCs outstanding increased from 15 percent to 35 percent of total C&I loans during this period.[7]

2.2. Payoff Characteristics

It is useful when analyzing the reasons for loan sales and SLC issues to begin by evaluating the payoff or cash flow characteristics of these transactions. Consider first a loan sale with recourse. The loan sold is the primary source of cash flows to the purchaser. In the event of default on the loan, the purchaser will receive the contracted payment as long as the selling bank does not fail. In the event that the bank fails, the purchaser receives any cash flows from the loan sold plus a general claim on the bank's other assets. In a loan sale without recourse, the loan sold is the sole source of cash flows to the purchaser.

An SLC-backed loan operates in a similar fashion. The primary source

---

is repeatedly in the market, reputational capital may assure quality (see Gorton and Haubrich [1987]). A second technique involves the sale of short-term strips of longer-term loans. Finally, because the selling bank is typically responsible for servicing the loan, the nature of the seller's liability in the event of default is uncertain.

6. See James (1987).

7. See Koppenhaver (1987) or James (1987).

of cash flows is the loan funded by the beneficiary. The lender (beneficiary) also receives a claim on the bank's assets in the event of a default on the loan. Therefore, just as in the case of a loan sale with recourse, the lender receives the minimum of the contracted rate on the SLC-backed loan or, in the event of default on the loan and the bank's failure, the cash flows from the loan plus a general claim on the bank's other assets.[8]

If the bank could issue uninsured deposits secured by a specific loan, precisely the same factors would determine the cash flows to secured depositors. Specifically, the secured depositor would receive less than the contracted payment only when the bank failed and the cash flows from the collateral were less than the contracted payments due on the debt.[9]

Loan sales with recourse and SLC-backed loans are therefore functionally equivalent to secured debt and will in the absence of transaction costs have the same contracted rate as secured debt.[10] The contracted rate on loans sold without recourse will differ from the contracted rate on secured debt by the additional default risk and the agency costs associated with the removal of the recourse provision (see note 5).

2.3. Rationale for Loan Sales and SLC Issues

Previous research on the loan sales and SLC issues has focused on regulation and deposit insurance as the primary motives for off-balance sheet activities. Pennacchi (1987), Greenbaum and Thakor (1987), and Benveniste and Berger (1987) argue that loan sales and SLC issues result from regulatory taxes such as reserve requirements and capital requirements. Although banks are assumed to have a comparative advantage in originating and servicing

8. It is interesting to note that although loan sales with recourse and SLC-backed loans have identical payoff characteristics, they are treated differently for purposes of calculating minimum capital requirements. In particular, SLCs currently are not included in the calculation of capital requirements; loan sales with recourse are. Under proposed risk-based capital standards, this inconsistency will be eliminated by including SLCs as a liability for the purpose of calculating minimum capital requirements. See Moulton (1987) for a description of the proposed capital guidelines.

9. The analysis in this paper assumes that secured debt, SLCs, and the recourse provision on loan sales provide a general claim on the bank's assets with the same priority as deposits. Loan sales with recourse and SLC-backed loans are therefore functionally equivalent to a senior secured claim.

10. See James (1987) for a formal proof of the equivalence of loan sales with recourse, SLC-backed loans, and secured debt. The analysis assumes that in the event of default priority rules will be adhered to. Warner (1977) finds that in bankruptcy proceedings of nonfinancial firms priority rules in many instances are not followed. Because insured commercial banks are not subject to the federal bankruptcy code, there is additional uncertainty concerning the treatment of collateral in the event of bankruptcy (see Hayes [1987]). An advantage of loan sales and SLC-backed loans is that because title to the collateral is transferred, there is no uncertainty concerning the priority of the purchaser's claim in the event of bankruptcy. Moreover, the purchaser need not wait until the conclusion of bankruptcy proceedings (or the bank's liquidation) to obtain access to the collateral.

loans; regulatory taxes, they argue, make it unprofitable for banks to fund certain types of loans. The regulatory tax hypothesis predicts that banks will sell loans for which their comparative advantage in origination and monitoring is least (i.e., loans to investment grade credits).

Flannery (1987) argues that capital-adequacy requirements and examination standards motivate loan sales by providing banks an incentive to fund loans in a single risk class. Banks therefore have an incentive to sell loans they originate in other risk classes. The novel implication of Flannery's model is that banks may have an incentive to sell loans in a number of different risk classes rather than just loans to investment grade credits.

An alternative hypothesis concerning how regulation and deposit insurance influence off-balance sheet activities is the moral hazard hypothesis (see, for example, Pyle [1985]). This hypothesis focuses on the incentives banks have to increase asset risk and financial leverage when deposit insurance is provided at a fixed price. Under existing regulation, SLCs are excluded from capital requirements. Therefore, by issuing an SLC, a bank can increase its financial leverage and enhance whatever subsidies it receives from the deposit insurer. In addition, by selling relatively low-risk loans and maintaining riskier loans in its portfolio, a bank can increase its asset risk and enhance the subsidy deposit insurance provides. The moral hazard hypothesis therefore predicts that off-balance sheet activities will increase bank risk.

The model developed in this paper demonstrates that the incentives banks have to issue SLCs or to sell loans are similar to the incentives nonbank firms have to issue secured debt. The collateralization hypothesis, discussed in detail in the next section, predicts that banks will engage in loan sales or will issue SLCs even in the absence of regulation and deposit insurance. However, my model also predicts that capital requirements and deposit insurance increase the incentives to issue collateralized claims. Therefore, my model complements the regulatory tax models of loan sales and SLC issues.

2.4. The Collateralization Hypothesis

Stulz and Johnson (1985) analyze the incentives nonfinancial firms have to issue secured debt. One hypothesis is that shareholders can effect a wealth transfer from unsecured debt holders by unexpectedly increasing the default risk on unsecured debt. By providing secured debt holders a higher priority claim to the cash flow of a subset of the firm's existing assets, unsecured debt holders are worse off. This argument is similar to the moral hazard hypothesis concerning the issuance of SLCs and loan sales. As Stulz and

Johnson point out, if this were the primary reason for the issuance of secured debt, unsecured debt would contain covenants prohibiting secured-debt issues. In banking, if the sole motive for issuing SLCs or selling loans were to effect a wealth transfer from the FDIC and uninsured claimants to bank stockholders, then uninsured depositors and subordinated debt holders would include covenants prohibiting these transactions. Moreover, the largest issuers of SLCs and sellers of loans are money center and large regional banks with the largest proportion of uninsured or partially insured deposits (see James [1987]).

An alternative hypothesis, referred to as the underinvestment hypothesis, is that the ability to issue secured debt can affect a firm's investment policy and therefore the size as well as the distribution of future cash flows. In particular, the ability to issue secured debt may enable the firm to undertake *new* investment opportunities that it would pass up if constrained to unsecured debt financing. This can occur when the firm has risky debt outstanding paying a contractually fixed rate. The promised payment on new unsecured debt will reflect the uncertainty concerning the cash flows of the firm's existing assets as well as the newly acquired asset. However, if secured debt is used to finance a new project, the promised payment will primarily reflect the risk associated with the new investment opportunity. If the new investment opportunity is relatively low-risk, the contracted rate on secured debt will be lower than the contracted rate that must be paid on unsecured debt issues. The lower contracted payments on secured debt implies that the wealth transfer from shareholders to existing debt holders will be less with secured debt financing than with unsecured debt financing. Therefore, the firm will undertake some projects using secured debt financing that it would pass up if constrained to issuing unsecured claims.

A similar argument can be made for the use of off-balance sheet activities by commercial banks. In the next section I show that if there exists an underinvestment problem with deposit financing and the contracted rate on collateralized claims is less than the rate that must be paid on new deposits, the issuance of a collateralized claim will reduce the transfer to existing depositors associated with the new investment project.

3. The Model

3.1. Assumptions and Notation

I assume a two-period framework in which a bank has at time $t = 0$ one "booked" loan with a face value of \$1 and an option to invest in a second loan requiring an investment of $1 at time $t = 0$. If the opportunity to make the loan is not undertaken at time $t = 0$, the option expires and is worthless. Both the existing loan and the loan prospect (if undertaken) pay off at time $t = 1$. The bank's booked loan is financed with a mixture of equity and deposits, with e and $1 - e$ representing the amount of equity and deposits used. All market participants are assumed to be risk-neutral. In addition, deposit and equity markets are assumed to be perfectly competitive. An important assumption in the analysis that follows is that the rate on existing deposits is fixed at the time the new loan opportunity must be undertaken. This assumption is required for the underinvestment problem to occur (see Myers [1977]).[11]

The booked loan is assumed to have payoff characteristics of $a_1(s)$, where s represents a given state of nature. For simplicity I assume s is distributed uniformly over the interval $[0,s]$. The new loan opportunity is assumed to have payoff characteristics of $a_2(s)$. In addition, the loan opportunity is assumed to have a positive net present value so that its expected cash flows exceed the risk-free rate r_f.

Assume initially that deposits are uninsured. (The effect of deposit insurance is discussed later.) If the new loan were financed by issuing deposits promising a payment of r_n, the realized payoff to new depositors in any state will be

$$\min\{r_n, \frac{r_n}{L_d} A(s)\} \tag{1}$$

where

$$L_d = r_d (1 - e) + r_n$$
r_d = the contracted rate on existing deposits
$A(s) = a_1(s) + a_2(s)$.

Assuming risk neutrality, the expected payoff to new depositors will equal the risk-free rate:

$$\int_0^s \min\{r_n, \frac{r_n}{L_d} A(s)\} f(s)\ ds = r_f. \tag{2}$$

Equations (1) and (2) reflect the fact that all depositors (both existing and new) have the same priority claim on the bank's assets.

---

11. For the underinvestment problem to arise, the rate on a portion of the firm's outstanding debt must be fixed. The use of short-term debt can reduce the underinvestment problem by increasing the frequency with which debt is repriced. However, an underinvestment problem can arise even if debt is repriced continuously if there exists an information asymmetry between managers and outside investors concerning the firm's investment opportunities.

3.2. The Underinvestment Problem

The bank will forgo the investment opportunity if constrained to deposit financing if the gains from undertaking the opportunity accrue primarily to existing depositors. Specifically, the bank will not undertake the loan if

$$
\int_0^s a_2(s)\, f(s)ds \; - \int_0^s \min\{r_n, \frac{r_n}{L_d} A(s)\}\, f(s)ds \; -[\int_0^s \min\{r_d\,(1-e),
$$

$$
\frac{r_d}{L_d} A(s)\}\, f(s)ds \; - \int_0^s \min\{r_d\,(1-e), a_1(s)\} f(s)ds] \le 0. \tag{3}
$$

Expression (3) represents the change in shareholder wealth resulting from investing in the new loan. The term in brackets represents the change in the value of existing deposits as a result of funding the loan. If the bracketed term is greater than zero, existing depositors gain from the bank's investment (either through a reduction in the probability of default or through an increase in the level of cash flows in the default states). Notice that because the new investment opportunity is assumed to have a positive net present value, the first term in (3) is greater than zero. In addition, because new deposits are assumed to be fairly priced when issued, the second term equals the risk-free rate. Therefore, (3) will be less than zero only if the term in brackets is greater than zero (i.e., depositors gain from the bank's investment).

Intuitively, the gain existing depositors realize reduces the return bank shareholders receive from the new loan and therefore reduces their incentives to undertake the loan. This transfer results in the underinvestment problem identified by Myers (1977).

The following proposition describes how issuing collateralized claims affects shareholder wealth.

Proposition 1. If there exists a wealth transfer from shareholders to existing depositors associated with financing a new loan and if the promised payment on collateralized claims is less than promised payment on new deposits, the issuance of collateralized claims will reduce the wealth transfer from shareholders to depositors.

This result can be derived as follows. First, note that if the new loan is sold with recourse (or used as collateral for a secured debt issue or backed by an SLC), then the realized payoffs to the purchaser in any given state is

$$\min\{r_s, a_2(s) + a_1(s) \frac{r_s}{L_s}\} \tag{4}$$

where r_s is the promised payment to the purchaser of the loan and L_s equals the sum of the contracted payments to the loan purchaser and existing depositors. If the loan sale is without recourse, the payoff to the purchaser is simply

$$\min\{r_s, a_2(s)\}. \tag{5}$$

By comparing the payoff characteristics of new deposits (expression (1)) to the payoff characteristics of a loan sale (expressions (4) and (5)), one can determine when the rate paid to the purchaser of the loan will be less than the rate on deposits. Specifically, if investors are risk-neutral, r_s will be less than r_n if and only if (1) there is a probability of the bank, failing if deposit financing is used (i.e., deposits are risky) and (2) in the event of default the cash flows the purchaser of the loan receives are larger than the cash flows new depositors receive. That is, for any given bankruptcy state with deposit financing,

$$\min\{r_s, a_2(s) + a_1(s) \frac{r_s}{L_s}\} > \min\{r_n, \frac{r_n}{L_d} A(s)\} \tag{6}$$

or for a nonrecourse sale

$$\min\{r_s, a_2(s)\} > \min\{r_n, \frac{r_n}{L_d} A(s)\}.$$

Intuitively, if investors are risk-neutral, the expected return on deposits and on the loan sale will be equal. For the contracted rate on the loan sale to be less than the rate paid on new deposits, the purchaser of the loan must expect higher payments in the event that the bank fails.

The conditions under which the contracted rate on a loan sale is less than the rate on deposit financing are also the conditions required for the use of loan sales or secured-debt claims to reduce the underinvestment problem. This can be shown by comparing the payoffs to existing depositors when loans are sold or secured debt is issued with the payoffs to depositors when new deposits are issued. If the new loan is financed by issuing a collateralized claim, the payoff to existing depositors in a given state is

$$\min\{r_d(1 - e), \max [\frac{r_d}{L_s} a_1(s), a_2(s) + a_1(s) - r_s]\} \tag{7}$$

for a sale with recourse and

$$\min\{r_d(1 - e), \max[a_1(s), a_2(s) + a_1(s) - r_s]\} \qquad (8)$$

for a sale without recourse.

Loan sales or secured-debt issues will reduce the underinvestment problem if

$$\min\{r_d (1 - e), \frac{r_d}{L_d} A(s)\} >$$

$$\min\{r_d(1 - e), \max [\frac{r_d}{L_s} a_1(s), a_2(s) + a_1(s) - r_s]\} \qquad (9)$$

for a claim with recourse and

$$\min\{r_d (1 - e), \frac{r_d}{L_d} A(s)\} >$$

$$\min\{r_d (1 - e), \max[a_1(s), a_2(s) + a_1(s) - r_s]\} \qquad (10)$$

for a claim without recourse.

Expressions (9) and (10) will hold only if the contracted rate on the loan sale is less than the rate on new deposits. To see this, note that in all states in which default does not occur, the payoffs will be the same to existing depositors whether deposits or secured debt is used. If the contracted rate on the loan sale or secured debt is less than the promised payments to new depositors, then in the default states the payments to loan purchasers or secured debt holders will be greater than the payments to new depositors. However, this implies that in these states the payments to existing depositors will be less. Therefore, (9) and (10) hold.

3.3. Capital Requirements and Deposit Insurance

Capital requirements and deposit insurance can exacerbate the underinvestment problem. For example, if capital regulation requires a new loan to be financed with at most $1 - e$ of deposits, then the increase in the value of existing deposits is larger. In particular, the value of existing deposits when $1 - e$ of new deposits are issued to finance the investment opportunity is

$$\int_0^s \min\{r_d(1 - e), \frac{r^d}{L_e} A(s)\} f(s) \, ds$$

where

$$L_e = (1 - e)r_d + (1 - e)r_n.$$

Because L_e is strictly less than L_d (the contracted obligations to depositors when the new loan is financed with all deposits), binding capital requirements increase the transfer to existing depositors. Moreover, if new equity is fairly priced when issued, then the first two terms in (3) are no larger when equity financing is used. Therefore, shareholders are worse off when binding capital requirements are imposed.

Intuitively, capital requirements prohibit the bank from offsetting a reduction in asset risk with an increase in financial risk. An increase in capital requirements is therefore expected to increase a bank's incentives to issue collateralized claims.

Fixed-price deposit insurance can also exacerbate the underinvestment problem. The underinvestment problem arises when a firm has existing debt outstanding paying a contractually fixed rate. If the rate paid on existing debt adjusts to fully reflect the marginal contribution of a new investment opportunity to the firm's overall asset risk, there will be no wealth transfer from shareholders to existing debt holders. With fixed-rate deposit insurance, the rate paid on existing deposits plus the insurance premium is invariant to changes in bank risk. Indeed, with 100 percent insurance the cost of deposits will not adjust at all to changes in asset risk.[12] Therefore, banks with risky deposits outstanding will tend to underinvest in relatively low-risk loans and overinvest in high-risk loans.

4. Empirical Implications

The model developed in Section 3 establishes that there are some loans that the bank will not undertake when constrained to deposit financing that will be undertaken if collateralized claims can be issued. This implies that bank depositors are not necessarily worse off when loans are sold or SLCs are issued.

The analysis presented in Section 3 also provides insights into when one would expect SLCs and loan sales to be used. Assume, for the moment, the sole motive for issuing SLCs or selling loans is to reduce the underinvestment problem. First, the underinvestment problem is not likely to be serious when a bank's deposits are not very risky. Therefore, the volume of loan sales and SLCs is expected to increase with the default risk of deposits. Specifically, SLCs and loan sales are expected to be used more

---

12. For an underinvestment problem to arise with 100 percent insurance, the rate paid on deposits plus the deposit insurance premium and the cost of maintaining reserves must exceed the risk-free rate.

frequently by banks with greater leverage and greater asset risk. Recent studies by James (1987) and Benveniste and Berger (1987) find the volume of SLCs issued and loans sold to be positively related to bank asset risk and financial leverage. In addition, Pavel (1988) finds that banks with the highest risk-deposit liabilities are the largest sellers of commercial loans.

Second, the underinvestment problem is not likely to be a serious problem for high-NPV loans or high-risk loans. Thus, loan sales and SLCs are likely to be used more frequently for low-risk loans to customers with a small amount of bank-specific capital (i.e., loans to investment-grade borrowers). The institutional arrangements are consistent with this prediction of my model. For example, the Federal Reserve's Lending Practices Survey for February 1986 found that approximately two-thirds of the loans sold by respondents were obligations of investment-grade credits. Moreover, several studies have found default rates on SLC-backed loans to be lower than for commercial loans (see, for example, Benveniste and Berger [1986] and Goldberg and Lloyd-Davies [1985]).

Finally, because binding capital requirements can exacerbate the underinvestment problem, banks at or below the minimum primary capital requirement of 6 percent are expected to be the most active issuers of loan sales and SLCs. Recent studies by Benveniste and Berger (1987), James (1987), and Pavel and Phillis (1987) find that banks at or below the minimum capital requirement issue a larger volume of loan sales and SLCs than do banks with nonbinding capital requirements.

5. Summary and Conclusion

The model developed in this paper demonstrates that loan sales and SLC issues can avoid an underinvestment problem when a bank has risky deposits outstanding. I show that SLCs and loan sales can, like secured debt, reduce the underinvestment problem by permitting a bank to sell claims to a portion of the payoffs on new loans that would otherwise accrue to existing depositors. Therefore, the ability to issue collateralized claims will affect a bank's investment policy.

Because the ability to issue secured-debt substitutes can increase a bank's value, regulation designed to limit these activities can prove counterproductive and can result in an increase in the risk borne by the FDIC. More generally, the analysis suggests that regulations that restrict the type of financing used by the banks (e.g., capital requirements) and are intended to limit the FDIC's risk exposure may have the unintended effect of altering bank investment decisions and increasing the FDIC's risk exposure. By demonstrating that bank investment policy is related to financial policy, the model indicates that capital requirements, early closure rules, and other restrictions on financial policy can affect bank lending decisions.

REFERENCES

Bennett, Barbara. 1986. "Off Balance Sheet Risk in Banking: The Case of Standby Letters of Credit." San Francisco Federal Reserve Bank *Economic Review*, no. 1, pp. 19–29.

Benveniste, Lawrence, and Allen Berger. 1986. "An Empirical Analysis of Standby Letters of Credit." Working paper.

————. 1987. "Standby Letters of Credit: Benefits of Financing Loans off a Bank's Balance Sheet." Working paper.

Flannery, Mark. 1987. "Deposit Insurance, Capital Requirements and the Choice of Bank Loan Default Rates." Working paper.

Goldberg, Michael, and Peter Lloyd-Davies. 1985. "Standby Letters of Credit: Are Banks Overextending Themselves?" *Journal of Bank Research* 16, pp. 28–39.

Gorton, Gary, and Joseph Haubrich. 1987. "Loan Sales, Recourse and Reputation: An Analysis of Secondary Loan Participations." University of Pennsylvania, working paper.

Greenbaum, Stuart, and Anjan Thakor. 1987. "Bank Funding Modes: Securitization versus Deposits." Northwestern University Banking Research Center, working paper No. 146.

Hayes, David C. 1987. "Some Issues in Asset Securitization by National Banks." *Issues in Bank Regulation* 10, pp. 5–24.

James, Christopher. 1987. "The Use of Loan Sales and Standby Letters of Credit by Commercial Banks." University of Oregon, working paper.

Koppenhaver, Gary. 1987. "Standby Letters of Credit." Federal Reserve Bank of Chicago *Economic Perspectives* 11, pp. 28–35.

Melvin, Donald. 1986. "A Primer for RMA Staff on Legal and Regulatory Concepts and Standards in the Securitization of Loans." Robert Morris Associates, Philadelphia, Penn.

Moulton, Janice. 1987. "New Guidelines for Bank Capital." Federal Reserve Bank of Philadelphia *Business Review*, pp. 19–31.

Myers, Stewart. 1977. "Determinants of Corporate Borrowing." *Journal of Financial Economics* 5, pp. 147–175.

Pavel, Christine, and David Phillis. 1987. "Why Commercial Banks Sell Loans: An Empirical Analysis." Federal Reserve Bank of Chicago *Economic Perspectives* 11, pp. 16–31.

Pavel, Christine. 1988. "Loan Sales Have Little Effect on Bank Risk." Federal Reserve Bank of Chicago *Economic Perspectives* 12, pp. 23–31.

Pennacchi, George. 1987. "Loan Sales and the Cost of Bank Capital." University of Pennsylvania, working paper.

Pyle, David. 1985. "Discussion of Off Balance Sheet Banking." In *Search for Financial Stability: The Past Fifty Years*. San Francisco Federal Reserve Bank.

Stulz, Rene, and Herb Johnson. 1985. "An Analysis of Secured Debt." *Journal of Financial Economics* 7, pp. 117–161.

Warner, Jerold. 1977. "Bankruptcy, Absolute Priority and the Pricing of Risky Debt Claims." *Journal of Financial Economics* 4, pp. 329–350.

Are Loan Sales Really Off–Balance Sheet?

GARY GORTON* AND GEORGE PENNACCHI*

A commercial loan sale or secondary loan participation is a contract under which a bank sells the cash stream from a loan to a third party, usually without recourse. In accordance with accepted accounting procedures, this no-recourse contract allows removal of the underlying loan from the balance sheet of the bank, so that the funding of the loan is not subject to capital or reserve requirements. Since commercial banks are thought to specialize in the origination of nonmarketable claims on borrowing firms, the apparent ability of banks to sell these assets seems paradoxical. The paradox could be explained if loan sales contracts contained implicit guarantees in the form of options by loan buyers to sell the loans back to the bank if the underlying borrower performs worse than anticipated. If such guarantees exist, then loans that are sold represent contingent liabilities, and a rationale for increasing capital requirements may exist. As an indirect test of the existence of this guarantee, we investigate whether loan sales and commercial paper prices contain a risk premium for the default of the selling bank. The empirical evidence supports the hypothesis of implicit guarantees.

I. Introduction

Many contingent contracts of banks are not recorded on their balance sheet and are referred to as ''off–balance sheet items.'' A large number of important bank financial services fall into this category. Examples include loan commitments and lines of credit, standby and commercial letters of credit, financial futures and forward contracts, and interest rate and foreign currency swaps. Under these contracts the bank explicitly creates a contingent asset or liability, usually in exchange for a fee. In the past fifteen years

*Department of Finance, The Wharton School, University of Pennsylvania.

The first author thanks the Geewax-Terker Research Program in Financial Instruments for research support. The authors appreciate the assistance of Andrew Albert of *Asset Sales Report*. The research assistance of Sung-ho Ahn, Arvind Krishnamurthy, and Robin Pal is greatly appreciated. Errors remain the authors'.

the volume of such off–balance sheet activity has grown enormously relative to the volume of "on–balance sheet" activity such as loan creation.[1]

Another recent activity of banks that has increased rapidly appears to resemble these off–balance sheet activities. The new activity is the practice of selling loans. A commercial loan sale is a contract between a bank and a third party under which the bank sells the cash stream from a commercial loan to the third party, in most cases without explicit recourse, guarantees, insurance, or any other type of credit enhancement. Since the contract selling the cash stream from the loan explicitly states that the sale is without recourse, there appears to be no contingency under which the sale creates a liability for the bank. Unlike the traditional off–balance sheet activities in which the bank is at risk because a contingent liability is created, a loan sale appears to permanently and irrevocably remove the loan from the balance sheet. Thus, loan sales appear to be a unique form of off–balance sheet activity.

Actually, loan sales per se are not new. Banks have sold loans to other banks in the past. But three recent trends make this activity of singular importance to banking. First, the volume of loans sold has increased dramatically. According to FDIC Call Report data, the volume has increased from $23 billion in 1983 to $111 billion in 1986, an increase of 382 percent. The first quarter of 1987 alone saw $85 billion of loans sold. Prior to 1983 the volume of loans sold was not reported to the FDIC because the amount of loan sales activity was so small. An increasing number of banks are becoming involved in loan sales as buyers and as sellers. It is now commonplace for banks to have established asset sales groups. Second, unlike the traditional loan sales, an increasing amount of loans are now being sold to buyers who are not in the U.S. correspondent banking network; they are foreign banks, other intermediaries, and nonfinancial firms. (See Gorton and Haubrich [1987] for a review of the available data on loan sales.)

Finally, banks have actively sought to modify relationships with underlying borrowers in order to facilitate loan sales in such a way as to get the loans off the balance sheet, thereby avoiding funding costs associated with required reserves and capital.[2] Regulatory accounting procedures re-

---

1. The off–balance sheet activity that has attracted the most attention is the issuance of standby letters of credit. In June 1982 outstanding standby letters of credit amounted to $80.0 billion. In June 1985 the outstanding amount of standby letters of credit had grown to $153.2 billion, a 90 percent increase. (See Bennett [1986]; Wolkowitz et al. [1982].)

2. Pennacchi (1988) analyzes banks' incentives for selling or buying loans based on regulatory costs and their degree of deposit market competition. Optimal contractual arrangements between loan buyers and sellers are also examined under the assumption that banks provide monitoring services. Flannery (1988), Greenbaum and Thakor (1987), and James (1987a) present additional motives for bank loan sales.

quire that for the underlying loan to be removed from the balance sheet, the loan sale must not only involve no recourse, but must also be sold on the same terms and conditions as the original, underlying loan was made. In other words, the loan sale must be the same maturity and the same pricing mechanism, (i.e., fixed or floating in the same way), as the underlying loan.[3] This has meant, in practice, alterations of contractual relations with borrowers.[4] Borrowers must be convinced, for example, to take shorter-maturity loans with implicit promises of rollover instead of explicit longer-maturity loans because the buyers of loans have shown a preference for shorter maturities. Hence, long-term customer relationships and longer contract lengths are being modified, significantly altering the way in which banking is conducted.

The ability of banks to create loans and then resell them without recourse in significant amounts appears to contradict the essence of banking. Theoretical rationales for the existence of banks predict that loans will be nonmarketable securities. The basic argument runs as follows. In a world in which there are information asymmetries between borrowers and lenders, banks perform some service that market participants cannot produce. Examples of such services include bank production of information about borrowers' potential investment opportunities or monitoring of borrowers' investment activities by enforcing loan covenants.[5] Banks perform these services on behalf of market participants (e.g., depositors) who, in turn, can rely on banks because banks are at risk if they do not perform. Banks' incentive to perform these activities results from the disproportionate share of the loss suffered by bank equity holders from loan defaults caused by nonperformance. Consequently, this theoretical rationale would imply that bank assets would be nonmarketable. If market participants were willing to buy, without recourse, the claims on borrowers originated by banks, then those same market participants could have purchased these claims directly from borrowers to start with and there would be no need for banks.

How, then, can these loans be sold without recourse? One possibility is that the loans sold are claims on borrowers who do not require the information production and monitoring services traditionally provided via bank lending. Loan selling may really amount to underwriting in the same sense that underwriting is done by other financial intermediaries. In other

---

3. See Melvin (1986) for a more detailed discussion.

4. For example, the February 1986 Lending Practices Survey of the Federal Reserve System reported that 16.7 percent of all responding banks modified terms of revolving credit agreements to facilitate loan sales.

5. See Boyd and Prescott (1986), Diamond (1984), and Gorton and Haubrich (1986) for discussions of these bank activities.

words, there are no incentive problems between banks and loan buyers because the loans being sold are loans to companies that are very well known. In fact, however, whereas this seems to have been true in the early 1980s when loans began to be sold in significant volume, in 1985 (the only year for which such data are available) about a third of the loans sold were to companies that did not have access to the commercial paper market.[6] Consequently, this cannot be the full explanation. This suggests that there may be an alternative mechanism that makes loan sales incentive compatible. This mechanism might take the form of an implicit guarantee by the bank to buy the loans back from loan purchasers if certain events occur.

If the loan sales contract is mutually beneficial for the borrower, the bank, and the loan buyer only if it can be removed from the balance sheet in order to avoid costs of required reserves and capital, then in order to accomplish the sale, the contract must explicitly state that there is no recourse (to satisfy accounting regulations). However, in order for purchasers to be willing to buy loans, the bank may implicitly offer to guarantee the loans sold by agreeing to buy them back if there are unanticipated changes in the value of an underlying loan. Since the loans sold are not riskless, the guarantee must concern the difference between the buyer's perceived risk and subsequent realized risk. As a matter of course, banks buy loans back, although there are no data on the extent or price of such repurchases.[7] However, if these repurchases represent loan purchasers' exercise of implicit guarantees, then loan sales involve the creation of contingent liabilities similar to other off-balance sheet contracts.

If banks are selling loans with this implicit guarantee, then they may be providing a service similar to a back-up line of credit (loan commitment) provided by commercial banks when firms issue commercial paper. Under this hypothesis, loan sales represent a substitute for commercial paper underwritten with a back-up credit line. Since banks have been restricted from underwriting, loan sales might be a way for them to jointly underwrite and issue a contingent liability similar to a credit line. Hence, if proposals are implemented that seek to make a bank's required capital a function of its volume of credit lines, consistency might imply that required capital also depends on a bank's loan sales volume.

In this paper we empirically investigate whether loan sales contracts contain implicit guarantees of a magnitude similar to the more-explicit guarantees represented by lines of credit backing commercial paper. If such

---

6. See the June 1985 Lending Practices Survey of the Federal Reserve System.

7. This statement summarizes impressions from conversations with asset sales bankers at money center banks.

guarantees exist, then loan and commercial paper purchasers would be concerned with the default risk of the bank providing the guarantee, because the bank's ability to make good on the guarantee depends on its solvency. For example, if an implicit guarantee exists when a loan is sold, the risk premium on the loan sold should, at least in part, reflect the bank's default risk. Variation in the spread of yields of loan sales over a risk-free rate should reflect movements in the risk of default by the selling bank as well as the borrowing firm. We test for the presence of an implicit guarantee on loans sold by comparing the sensitivity to bank default risk of loan sales' risk premia relative to the risk premia on commercial paper.

The paper proceeds as follows. In Section II we briefly summarize the available information on loan sales as background and explain the data to be used for the empirical tests. In Section III the basis of the empirical tests is developed. The test results are reported and discussed in Section IV. Section V concludes.

II. Commercial Loan Sales Contracts and the Loan Sales Market

In this section commercial loan sales contracts are briefly reviewed and some stylized facts about the loan sales market are discussed. The loan sales price data, to be used subsequently, are introduced. Finally, the role of bank credit enhancements for commercial paper is discussed since we will be comparing these guarantees to possible guarantees on loan sales.

A. Loan Sales Contracts

A loan sale is a contract that sells the cash stream from a loan contract to a third party. The loan contract itself is not transferred. Rather, a new contract is created that commits the cash stream from a specified loan, for a specified period of time, to a third party. The commitment of this cash stream is sold to a "loan buyer" under a contract that states that the buyer has no recourse against the selling bank should the underlying bank borrower default, and since the loan sale contract is between the bank and the third party, the third-party buyer cannot directly negotiate with the underlying borrower, should the borrower default.

There are two kinds of commercial loan sales contracts: loan strips and loan participations.[8] A loan strip represents a short-term share of a longer-

---

8. Loans may also be transferred under more stringent contracts. An *assignment* is a contract under which a share of a credit is sold with all rights, but without full responsibilities to the borrowing company. A *novation* is a share of a credit sold with all voting rights and responsibilities that are included in the original loan contract. See Gorton and Haubrich (1987) for a more complete discussion.

term loan commitment. When the strip comes due at the end of a given period—say five, thirty, sixty, or ninety days—the selling bank has a commitment to resell the strip over the subsequent period or to provide funding for the loan itself. With a loan participation, a bank sells a loan to maturity without recourse. The date at which the loan sale matures coincides with the maturity date of the underlying loan.

The issue of whether loan sales involve an implicit guarantee or not most clearly arises when loans are sold under the loan participation contract. Since this contract involves no recourse and sells the loan to maturity, clearly once the loan is sold the bank is no longer explicitly at risk. Consequently, the incentives the bank faces may be different than if the loan was on the bank's books. The issue is more complicated, however, when loans are sold as strips. Strips expose the bank to the risk that it will have to fund the loan when the strip matures. Since the bank has made a commitment to resell the strip or provide funding itself, the bank is at risk when the strip matures. This means, for example, that a bank is less likely to shirk in information production or covenant monitoring during the life of the strip. It also implies that the risk may be similar to that faced by a bank when it provides a back-up line of credit on commercial paper.

The fact that strips expose the bank to refunding risk has raised the question of whether banks should be allowed to take loans off their balance sheets when they are sold under strips. The Financial Accounting Standards Board (FASB) offered a proposal in December 1987 that would require banks to account for risks assumed in selling loans. As a result, some banks are reported to have moved away from strips and to be concentrating on selling loans under the participation contract. In January 1988 the FASB decided that loan strips could be recorded as sales if (1) the buyer of the strip assumes the full risk of loss and (2) the lender has no contractual obligation to repurchase the loan strip.

Controversy has ensued over whether most loan strips satisfy these requirements. The banking committee of the American Institute of Certified Public Accountants (AICPA) announced (January 1988) that it considers a strip to be a sale if, at the strip's maturity, the original lender refuses to lend for one of two reasons: (1) if the borrower violates a covenant included in the loan contract or (2) if a material adverse change in the borrower's condition is discovered during a credit evaluation.[9] Condition 2 is similar to the condition frequently placed in loan commitment contracts that may be invoked to remove the bank's liability of providing the loan commitment. In practice, however, it seems that banks rarely utilize this condition to

---

9. Further details are provided in *Asset Sales Report,* January 25, 1988.

avoid funding a loan. Employing this condition may be at the expense of a loss in reputation as a reliable provider of loan commitments.

Similar to credit lines used to back up commercial paper, the issue of an implicit guarantee on a loan strip arises when the contract explicitly states that the bank has no obligation to buy the strip back and when it has no binding obligation to refund the loan when covenants are violated or the borrower's credit condition deteriorates. In this case the strip buyer cannot rely on the fact that the bank has made a longer-term (nonbinding) commitment to refund the loan, so the bank's incentive to maintain the value of the loan may be suspect. If the bank does not maintain the value of the loan, it can always choose not to refund the loan. In this case the issue of the implicit guarantee arises exactly as before.

In either case the buyer of the loan has no rights against the underlying borrower. If the underlying borrower defaults, the loan buyer must rely on the bank to represent it. To date there has been one known failure in the loan sales market. In this instance the bank invited the loan buyers along to the renegotiation sessions with the borrower, even though the loan buyers had no legal right to be there.[10] To some extent these incentive issues are mitigated if the bank does not sell the entire loan. Informally, banks indicate that they keep about 10 percent of each loan sold although there is no contractual obligation to do so.[11]

B. The Loan Sales Market

The commercial loan sales market is growing and changing so fast that it is difficult to adequately summarize recent developments. Gorton and Haubrich (1987) report the following stylized facts about the loan sales market:

1. The volume of loan sales has grown enormously in the past five years. (The Lending Practices Survey of the Board of Governors of the Federal Reserve System reported that the volume of loan sales over the first half of the fourth quarter of 1984 was $5 billion. In

10. The one failure involved Republic Health Corporation. In August 1986 Republic Health borrowed $265 million from a syndicate with Security Pacific as lead bank, and eight other lenders. Security Pacific sold part of its share of the loan. In July 1986 Republic Health stopped interest payments on the loan. According to *Asset Sales Report,* October 5, 1987: "Sources have reported that SecPac officials have been accompanied by representatives of a participating bank at several of Republic's workout meetings. The development was notable because investors in participations are considered non-voting members of the lending group, and therefore have virtually no influence at workout meetings."

11. This statement summarizes conversations with asset sales bankers at money center banks. Pennacchi (1988) solves for the optimal size of the claim that banks would choose to retain on a loan sold.

June 1985 the survey reported sales of $23.5 billion during the first two-thirds of the second quarter of 1985. By the fourth quarter of 1987 the comparable FDIC measure of volume was $85 billion.)

2. The number of banks selling loans has also increased. (Pavel and Phillis [1987] report that 3,214 banks reported selling loans in each of the four quarters of 1985.)

3. A significant portion of the loans sold are merger-related. (The Lending Practices Survey of the Federal Reserve system reported in March 1987 that ''over one-third of all loans sold or participated in 1986 were merger-related.'')

4. A significant portion of the loans sold are bought by foreign banks. (The Lending Practices Survey reported in June 1985 that foreign banks bought 60 percent of total loans sold.)

5. A typical borrower profile for a loan sold would be a U.S. corporation that has publicly traded debt rated Baa or better and has commercial paper rated A1/P1 or A2/P2. (The June 1985 Lending Practices Survey reported that 68 percent of loans sold were to firms with access to the commercial paper market.)

6. Loan maturities range from one day to two years, but tend to be of shorter maturity. (The Lending Practices Survey of June 1985 reported that 80 percent of loans sold had maturities of 90 days or less.)

Loans that are sold have most often been originated in the usual way (i.e., a bank customer borrows money). Then the loan is sold to the third party. But loan sales also increasingly seem to be arising from the ''bid business'' in which banks that are members of large, syndicated revolving credit agreements bid for a share of the credit when the customer wants a loan. When the customer is ready to draw down a credit, a member bank can bid for the entire loan or a piece of the loan. The borrower is obligated to take the lowest bid and the winning bank then typically sells the loan. The bid business combined with loan sales most closely resembles underwriting behavior.

C. Loan Sales Data

Data on prices of loans sold are scarce. The data used in this study are from *Asset Sales Report,* a weekly industry publication that has been in existence since late July 1987. To our knowledge this is the only available data on prices of loans sold.[12]

---

12. No bank we contacted was willing to provide any data on loan sales.

Asset Sales Report collects "average yields on short-term loans offered to investors by Bankers Trust, Citibank, and Security Pacific." Yields on loan sales of three maturities are reported: five-day, thirty-day, and ninety-day. Also, for each maturity the banks report yields for the loans to borrowers with commercial paper programs rated A1/P1 and A2/P2. Thus, there is no information on loans sold which were to underlying borrowers that do not issue commercial paper (i.e., are not publicly traded). *Asset Sales Report* informs us that there is little variation in yields across the reporting banks they survey. Of the three banks in their survey, Citibank and Bankers Trust are the largest loan sellers. Citibank had loan sales of $23.142 billion in the first quarter of 1987 according the FDIC Call Report data; Bankers Trust sold over $20 billion. Security Pacific was the sixth largest seller of loans with $3.05 billion of loan sales. Citibank accounted for 27 percent of the volume reported by the top twenty-five loan-selling banks during this quarter.

D. Banks and Commercial Paper

Commercial paper issuance typically requires some kind of credit enhancement, usually from a bank. The credit enhancement may take the form of an explicit guarantee such as an irrevocable revolving credit, a standby letter of credit, an insurance company indemnity bond, or a direct pay commitment. Or the credit enhancement may be a less formal loan commitment.

Almost all commercial paper issuers maintain 100 percent backing for their paper in one of these forms. For example, Calomiris (no date) reports that "of the more than 1400 commercial paper issuers listed in the December 1986 Standard and Poor's *Commercial Paper Rating Guide,* only 59 reported backup lines of less than 100 percent." Rating agencies require that the backup lines be confirmed in writing in order to be taken into consideration for rating the firm's paper. Oral commitments are not sufficient.[13]

Although backup lines must be confirmed in writing to the rating services, they can be fairly informal. The Federal Reserve System, in Statistical Release G-21 (discontinued since August 5, 1987), reports data on four categories of loan commitments: "term," "revolving," and "other" formal arrangements; and informal "confirmed lines" which do not involve specific interest rates or advance fees. According to the Fed, confirmed lines of credit "represent general expressions of willingness to lend, other than for

---

13. Thus, according to Bates (1986), writing in Standard and Poor's weekly: "To be viewed as eligible, back-up lines must be confirmed in writing. An oral commitment is not sufficient" (quoted by Calomiris).

term loans or revolving credits, that are made known to the customer but are not characterized by detailed formal agreements specifying the terms and conditions under which a loan is made."[14] Calomiris presents econometric evidence confirming the informal industry view that, among credit lines, confirmed lines are most closely linked to commercial paper.

There is little evidence on the extent to which commercial paper is backed by explicit guarantees versus the less-formal guarantees. The 1985 Lending Practices Survey reported that 11 percent of the outstanding standby letters of credit were issued to back taxable commercial paper. That amount ($13.6 billion) represented approximately 18 percent of the outstanding commercial paper of nonfinancial firms at that time. Thus, it seems that formal guarantees account for a significant amount of the backing.

Whether the backing is formal or not, it represents an option that matures at the date the commercial paper matures. The value of this option depends on the default risk of the bank providing the backing. It is not surprising, then, that Standard and Poor's, for example, requires the bank providing the credit enhancement to be rated A2 or better. However, these credit enhancements are European options. In the case of loan sales, the informal or implicit offer to repurchase the loan at the demand of the loan buyer would be an American option. This distinction plays an important role later.

III. Investigating an Implicit Guarantee by the Loan-Selling Bank

In this section, we propose a way to investigate the proposition that banks selling loans provide implicit recourse to the buyers of loans. An indirect test of this proposition can be carried out by estimating the magnitude of the implicit guarantee given on loan sales relative to the magnitude of the guarantee given by banks when providing backup lines of credit on commercial paper.

A. Simple Model of the Yields on Loans Sold and Commercial Paper

The yields on loans sold and commercial paper are assumed to be a function of three factors: (1) the opportunity cost of funds to loan buyers and commercial paper holders, (2) the risk of the firm issuing the loan or commercial paper, and (3) the quality of the guarantee given by the bank

---

14. Term loan commitments, according to the Federal Reserve System, are commitments for a term loan of original maturity greater than one year. Revolving credits are commitment agreements that allow repeated borrowing and repaying without penalty. The remaining category, "other," is those detailed, formal agreements that do not fall into one of the above categories.

to buy back the loan sold or provide a backup credit line in the case of commercial paper. The quality of this guarantee will depend on the default (failure) risk of the bank.

Consider the following model of the yield on a firm's debt security that may be partially guaranteed by a bank:

$$y_{jt} - r_t = \alpha_{j0} + \alpha_{j1}f_t + \alpha_{j2}b_t + \epsilon_{jt}, \qquad j = 1,c. \qquad (1)$$

y_{jt} is the yield on a debt security of type j issued at time t, where $j = 1,c$ indexes a loan (1) or an issue of commercial paper (c). r_t is the opportunity cost of an equivalent maturity riskless investment at time t. f_t is a measure of the default risk of the borrowing firm, and b_t is a measure of the default risk of the bank providing the guarantee on the security. The α_{ji}'s, $i = 0,1,2$, are constants, and ϵ_{jt} is an independently distributed error term.

Merton (1974) derives the spread between a firm's risky (nonguaranteed) debt and a risk-free rate as a function of the borrowing firm's leverage and the variance of its asset returns. In our model, this spread is represented by the variable f_t. In the more general case in which a bank may provide some partial guarantee on this debt, we would expect that the coefficient α_{j1} would be less than 1, and the smaller the stronger is the guarantee made by the bank. In the limit, if the bank's guarantee is believed to be completely certain (and the bank itself is perceived to have a zero probability of failure), then the coefficient α_{j1} would be zero.

The bank's guarantee will be limited by the likelihood of the bank's failure, which will depend on the bank's leverage and its variance of asset returns. A risk premium corresponding to this probability of failure is measured by the variable b_t. Thus, if a bank gives at least a partial option to loan buyers to repurchase loans sold, one would expect that α_{12} would be positive, whereas if a bank has some commitment to provide a backup credit line on commercial paper, then α_{c2} should be positive. These coefficients will be larger the greater the belief by investors that the bank will choose to uphold its guarantee. In summary, a substantial bank guarantee would imply a small value of the coefficient multiplying f_t and a large value of the coefficient multiplying b_t, whereas the reverse would be true if the bank's guarantee was weak.

B. Empirical Method

Ideally we would like to estimate the model in Equation (1) to test whether the guarantees given by banks on loans sold or commercial paper are substantial. Unfortunately, our time series data on yields on loans sold is not disaggregated at the individual borrowing firm level but is an average of yields of loans to borrowers who also issue a given grade of commercial paper, A1/P1 or A2/P2. This makes obtaining a relevant direct measure of the borrowing firm's risk f_t quite difficult. However, since we know these borrowers are issuers of commercial paper of a specific grade, we can jointly use the data on loan sales yields and commercial paper yields to test the *relative* strengths of guarantees given by banks selling loans versus providing backup credit lines on commercial paper. In order to do this, we assume that the banks providing the loan sales guarantees are the same or very similar in terms of their default risk to the banks providing the backup credit lines for the commercial paper. In that case, the variable b_t in Equation (1) can be assumed to be the same for both loan sales and commercial paper.

Under these assumptions, we can substitute out for the variable f_t in the loan sales equation using its value implied by the commercial paper equation to obtain:

$$y_{lt} - r_t = \alpha_{10} - \alpha_{c0}\alpha_{11}/\alpha_{c1} + (\alpha_{11}/\alpha_{c1})(y_{ct} - r_t)$$
$$+ (\alpha_{12} - \alpha_{c2}\alpha_{11}/\alpha_{c1})b_t + \epsilon_{lt} - (\alpha_{11}/\alpha_{c1})\epsilon_{ct}. \quad (2)$$

Equation (2) is the regression equation that forms the basis of our empirical tests. We now describe the method used to calculate the bank risk variable b_t.

C. Calculation of a Premium for Bank Risk

The premium for bank risk that we choose is one that is proportional to the premium that an uninsured bank depositor would charge the bank. To see how this might proxy for a relevant risk measure, suppose that a loan purchased by a loan buyer has a probability equal to p of being paid in full by the borrowing firm, and thus a probability of $(1 - p)$ of the borrowing firm's defaulting. If the bank had guaranteed the loan and the borrowing firm does indeed default, then the loan buyer might have a liability claim on the bank. If we assume that this claim is of equal claimant status to an uninsured bank depositor (i.e., a general creditor of the bank), then only partial payment of the loan buyer's promised claim would be made. This would suggest that $(1 - p)$ times the uninsured depositor's risk premium would be a relevant bank risk premium for the loan buyer. Employing the simplifying assumptions that the maturity date of the uninsured deposits and the auditing date of the FDIC coincide, and assuming that the FDIC's deposit insurance premium is fair, we can compute this risk premium in a manner similar to that of Merton (1974, 1977):

$$b_t = N(-d_2) - x_t N(-d_1) \qquad (3)$$

where $d_1 = (\ln x_t + \sigma^2\tau/2)/\sigma\sqrt{\tau}$; $d_2 = (d_1 - \sigma\sqrt{\tau})$; and $N(z)$ is the probability that a normally distributed random variable with mean zero and variance of unity will be less than or equal to z. x_t is the ratio of the market value of the bank's assets to the promised payment on its liabilities at time t, σ is the (assumed constant) standard deviation of the rate of return on the bank's assets, and τ is the time to maturity of the deposit. Note that in order to directly calculate this premium, one would need to observe values for x_t, the ratio of the market value of the bank's assets to its liabilities, and σ, the standard deviation of asset rates of return. Rather than attempt to directly calculate these variables, we choose to follow a procedure similar to Marcus and Shaked (1984) that calculates these variables using information contained in bank stock prices.

Note that the equilibrium value of the bank's equity per dollar liability, e_t, and the standard deviation of the return on bank equity, σ_{et}, are given by:

and

$$e_t = x_t N(d_1) - N(d_2) \qquad (4)$$

$$\sigma_{et} = \sigma x_t N(d_1)/[x_t N(d_1) - N(d_2)]. \qquad (5)$$

If we can observe the market value of the bank's equity per dollar liability, e_t, and calculate its standard deviation of returns, σ_{et}, then equations (4) and (5) represent two equations in two unknowns, x_t and σ. A numerical minimization algorithm can be employed to solve for these two unknowns. Since we can observe a different market value of equity, e_t, at each point in time over our sample period, we can carry out this numerical procedure to obtain an (x_t, σ_t) pair for each point in time.[15] However, since our model is based on the Black-Scholes-Merton assumption that the standard deviation of asset returns is constant over time, we use the average of the implied standard deviations to calculate a single implied standard deviation, σ. These values for x_t and σ can then be used to calculate a time series of premia for bank risk, b_t, given in equation (3).

IV. Empirical Investigation and Interpretation

Empirical tests of the model were carried out using weekly data over the period July 1987 to March 1988, a total of thirty-two observations. Since the reported weekly loan sales yields were an average of three different

---

15. Because of the relatively small sample size (thirty-two weekly observations), each (x_t, σ_t) pair was calculated based on the same estimate of σ_e.

TABLE 1

Summary Statistics of Variables

90-Day Bank Default Risk Premium	*Mean*	*Std. Deviation*
Bankers Trust	3.32×10^{-7}	6.54×10^{-7}
Citicorp	1.04×10^{-6}	2.01×10^{-6}
Security Pacific	4.25×10^{-8}	9.39×10^{-8}

Correlation Matrix of Risk Premia

1	.408	.730	Bankers Trust
.408	1	.388	Citicorp
.730	.388	1	Security Pacific

Implied Ratios of Market Values *of Bank Assets to Liabilities*	*Mean*	*Std. Deviation*
Bankers Trust	1.052	.0094
Citicorp	1.038	.0052
Security Pacific	1.048	.0057

Implied Standard Deviations of *the Returns of Bank Assets*	*Mean*	*Std. Deviation*
Bankers Trust	.0239	.0041
Citicorp	.0200	.0026
Security Pacific	.0205	.0023

Yield Spread over 90-Day LIBOR	*Mean*	*Std. Deviation*
(Difference between Annualized Yields)		
90-Day Loans Sold, A1/P1	$-.0006$	.2000
90-Day Commercial Paper, A1/P1	.2731	.2463
90-Day Loans Sold, A2/P2	.1302	.1930
90-Day Commercial Paper, A2/P2	.5308	.2390

banks—Bankers Trust, Citibank, and Security Pacific—we calculated a time series of the bank risk variable, b_t, which was a weighted average of the bank risk premia for the individual banks. The weights used equaled the ratio of the bank's volume of loan sales to the total volume for each of the three banks — 0.437, 0.498, 0.066, for Bankers Trust, Citibank, and Security Pacific, respectively. Table 1 gives the means, standard deviations, and correlation matrix of the ninety days-to-maturity bank risk premium variable for each of the three banks. The means and standard deviations of the banks' implied asset value to liability ratios, x, and standard deviation of asset returns, σ, are also reported.

Since the loan sales and commercial paper yields used in the estimation had a ninety-day maturity, we selected r_t to be the contemporaneous ninety-day London Interbank Offered Rate (LIBOR) yield. Since the majority of

TABLE 2

Correlations Between Yield Spreads and Bank Risk

OLS Regressions
July 1987 to March 1988, 32 Observations
(Standard Errors in Parentheses)

Dependent Variable	Independent Variables		R^2
Yield Spread $(Y_{jt} - r_t)$	Intercept	Bank Risk Premium $(f_t \times 10^6)$	
Loan Sold, A1/P1	−.0196 (.0411)	.0283 (.0312)	.027
Com. Paper, A1/P1	.2300 (.0489)	.0645 (.0371)	.091
Loan Sold, A2/P2	.1097 (.0395)	.0308 (.0300)	.034
Com. Paper, A2/P2	.4833 (.0467)	.0712 (.0355)	.118

loan purchasers are foreign and domestic banks, the LIBOR rate may be a good measure of loan buyers' opportunity cost of funds. Table 1 also presents summary statistics of the spread of loan sales yields and commercial paper over LIBOR, for both A1/P1 and A2/P2 rated borrowers.

A. Empirical Results

As a preliminary step in analyzing the data, we looked at the correlation between the spread on loan sales over LIBOR, $y_{1t} - r_t$, with the bank risk variable, b_t, and also the correlation between the spread on commercial paper over LIBOR, $y_{ct} - r_t$, with the bank risk variable. In other words, we ran the OLS regression given by equation (1) *leaving out* the (unobserved) firm default risk variable, f_t. Table 2 reports these results for both the A1/P1 rated and A2/P2 rated borrowers. In each of the four cases, the point estimates indicate positive correlation between the bank yield spreads on loans sold and the bank risk variable. However, only for the case of the A2/P2 rated commercial paper spread is the point estimate significantly different from zero at the 5 percent confidence level. If firm risk and bank risk, f_t and b_t, were uncorrelated, then our point estimates would be unbiased estimates of α_{j2}, but the estimated standard errors would be upward biased, perhaps explaining the insignificant t-statistics obtained (e.g., see Maddala [1977, p. 156]). However, it could well be that b_t and f_t are positively correlated, in which case our OLS estimates for α_{j2} would be upward biased as well.

TABLE 3

OLS Regressions Relating Loan Sales Yield Spread to Commercial Paper Yield Spread and Bank Risk Premium

July 1987 to March 1988, 32 Observations
(Standard Errors in Parentheses)

Dependent Variable		Independent Variables		R^2
Loan Sale Yield Spread $(y_{lt}-r_t)$	Intercept	Com. Paper Yield Spread $(y_{ct}-r_t)$	Bank Risk Premium $(f_t \times 10^6)$	
A1/P1 Borrowers	−.2053	.8070	−.0237	.924
	(.0154)	(.0435)	(.0093)	
A2/P2 Borrowers	−.2860	.8187	−.0276	.939
	(.0215)	(.0394)	(.0082)	

Table 3 reports the OLS estimates of the coefficients in equation (2), first for A1/P1 borrowers, then for A2/P2 borrowers. The coefficient estimates are surprisingly similar for the two sets of borrowers. The estimates for α_{l1}/α_{c1}, for the two quality levels, are 0.807 and 0.819, respectively. Both numbers are significantly different from 1.0 at the 5 percent confidence level. This would suggest that investors place *less* weight on borrowers' default risk in the case of loans sold relative to commercial paper issued. This would be consistent with the hypothesis that the strength of the guarantee given by banks on loans sold *exceeds* that given on commercial paper.

However, we obtain a seemingly conflicting set of negative estimates for $\alpha_{12} - \alpha_{c2}\alpha_{l1}/\alpha_{c1}$, equal to −.0237 and −.0276 for the two quality levels, respectively. Both numbers are significantly different from zero at the 5 percent significance level. Since $\alpha_{l1}/\alpha_{c1} < 1$, this result implies that $\alpha_{c2} > \alpha_{12}$, suggesting that investors are more concerned with the default risk of the bank when it gives a guarantee for commercial paper than when it gives a guarantee on a loan sold. This would seem to imply that a stronger guarantee is given on commercial paper than for a loan sold.

B. Interpretation of the Results

How can these apparently contradictory results be explained? Two non-mutually exclusive explanations would lead to the above empirical estimates. The first explanation implies that the relevant measure of bank risk, b_t, is effectively smaller in the case of loans sold relative to the case of commercial paper underwriting, even though the guarantee on loans sold may be stronger. The second explanation implies that the relevant measure of the borrower's risk, f_t, is effectively smaller in the case of loans sold relative to commercial paper underwriting. Both of these explanations are consistent with loan sales' having lower average spreads over LIBOR than do commercial paper issues (Table 1).

The first explanation is based on the idea that the implicit guarantees on loan sales and commercial paper may be fundamentally different because the guarantee on a loan sold may be thought of as an American option, whereas the guarantee on commercial paper is a European option. This distinction is especially important when combined with the fact that these options are *options with default risk,* referred to by Johnson and Stulz (1987) as "vulnerable" options. In other words, the banks writing these options may voluntarily or involuntarily default. A bank may voluntarily default by possibly invoking the loan commitment conditions regarding the violation of a loan covenant by the borrower or a "materially adverse change" in the borrower's condition. An involuntary default would be triggered by the failure of the bank itself. Johnson and Stulz show that vulnerable options have comparative static results that can be quite different from those of standard exchange traded options not subject to default by the seller. In particular, an American option can be valued significantly higher than a European option because the right to early exercise increases in value when the likelihood of default by the writer increases. This implies that the European option will be highly dependent on the default probability (risk) of the writer, whereas the American option will not. A holder of an "in the money" American option can choose to exercise the option before the writer's default risk becomes too great.

In the context of commercial paper guarantees and loan sale guarantees, note that the holder of commercial paper can call on the guarantor at the maturity date of the paper, *but not before.* Perhaps by the maturity date, the borrower has experienced a significant "material adverse change in condition" or violated a loan covenant enabling the bank to legally renege on its guarantee, or perhaps by maturity the bank itself is in financial difficulty. In contrast, with loan sales the loan buyer may have the right to sell the loan back to the bank at any time *on or before maturity*. For example, a loan purchaser may have the implicit option to sell the loan back to the bank at the first sign that the credit risk of the borrower or the credit risk of the bank has begun to deteriorate. This early exercise feature implies that the value of the guarantee given by the bank is greater in the case of loan sales than in the case of commercial paper, since it will be little affected by the bank's risk. This implies that the effective premium that loan sales buyers will place on bank risk, $\alpha_{12}b_t$, will be quite small relative to that for commercial paper buyers. This would explain the negative coefficient obtained for $(\alpha_{12} - \alpha_{c2}\alpha_{l1}/\alpha_{c1})$ even though α_{l1}/α_{c1} was found to be greater than one (Table 3).

Some casual evidence is consistent with the interpretation of the guarantee as an American put option. Because of securities laws, banks cannot allow a secondary market in loans sold to develop. All loan sales contracts prohibit resale of the loan. (See Gorton and Haubrich [1987].) Commercial paper does have a secondary market, albeit a thin one. In order to compete with commercial paper, banks may agree to buy back the loans so that buyers are not faced with possible illiquidity. Indeed, this is the reason bankers give for their loan repurchases. The repurchase price is subject to bargaining and is not simply adjusted for elapsed time. The possibility of an implicit guarantee enters when the repurchase price is agreed on. Since, to provide liquidity, the bank must be willing to buy back the loan at any time, the implicit guarantee would take the form of the bank's absorbing (at least part of) any possible credit deterioration that may have occurred by buying the loan back at a price favorable to the loan holder.

The second explanation is based on the hypothesis that banks may do a more efficient job of monitoring and verifying the credit of borrowers who sell loans relative to borrowers who issue commercial paper. This can result from banks' having greater exposure to refunding risk in the case of loans sold relative to the case of commercial paper underwriting. Suppose, for the moment, that in the case of a loan sale the underlying lending commitment between the bank and the borrowing firm was of a longer maturity than the loan sale contract. Then, at the maturity of the loan sale contract, the bank would again be at risk, not only to re-fund the loan for the subsequent period, but perhaps for a number of periods into the future. Consequently, knowing this, the bank would continue to efficiently monitor the loan and enforce loan covenants during the time of the loan sale just as if a long-term loan had been held by the bank (i.e., a loan with a maturity equal to the maturity of the lending commitment). As explained above, however, the bank would not be able to remove this loan from the balance sheet in this case. In order to remove the loan from the bank balance sheet, the longer maturity lending commitment must be shortened so that the loan sale and the explicit lending commitment by the bank mature at the same time.

If the underlying borrower can be convinced to take a shorter maturity loan *with the implicit understanding that the loan is longer term,* then the loan could be sold and removed from the balance sheet. Moreover, the loan buyer may rely on the fact that the loan is implicitly part of the longer-term customer relationship in such a way that the bank has an incentive to behave as if the loan were on its balance sheet. To minimize its refunding risk for all future periods of the lending commitment, the bank would have the incentive to more intensively verify the creditworthiness or to monitor the borrower than in the case of providing a back-up line of credit on commercial paper, where the bank's refunding risk lasts for only the single period subsequent to the maturity of the paper. This implies that for an equal maturity loan strip and commercial paper issue, the effective premium charged by a loan buyer to cover the default risk of the borrower would be less than that charged by the commercial paper holder (i.e., $\alpha_{ll}f_t < \alpha_{cl}f_t$). This would explain the estimated value of α_{ll}/α_{cl} in Table 3 being less than one.

In fact, Table 1 shows that the above hypotheses are quite reasonable. In Table 1 the means for ninety-day loan sales are *lower* than for ninety-day commercial paper for both qualities. The standard deviations for loan sales are also lower. The suggestion is that loan sales are less risky. Thus, loan sales must be safer because of some type of credit enhancement or borrowers happen to be safer or better monitored when they sell loans versus when they issue commercial paper.[16] The two interpretations suggested above are possible methods for banks to facilitate loan selling that make this activity significantly different from underwriting.

V. Conclusions

The fact that banks are selling loans under nonrecourse contracts in increasing amounts seems to contradict the unique role of banks as originators and holders of nonmarketable claims on firms. The ability of banks to sell loans could be explained if such sales involved implicit guarantees. We have investigated the existence of such guarantees relative to the better-understood guarantees that banks provide for commercial paper.

The empirical evidence is ambiguous. Although we can say that any guarantees that exist on loan sales are different from those backing commercial paper, we cannot distinguish between two, non-mutually exclusive, alternative ways for banks to guarantee the loans sold. The first explanation is that the bank offers a "vulnerable" American put option to the loan buyer. Since the bank itself is risky, this option is more valuable than a vulnerable European option. Since the option allows the loan buyer to sell the loan back before maturity, the bank is taking more risk than it would with a guarantee on commercial paper. We have not investigated what mechanism ensures loan buyers that this guarantee will, in fact, be adhered

---

16. This evidence is consistent with that found by James (1987b).

to, especially when the explicit contract definitively says that such guarantees do not exist.

Alternatively, the loan buyer, instead of relying on an option to force the bank to repurchase the loan, may rely on an underlying long-term bank relationship with the borrower. If such a relationship exists, implicitly, then the bank has an incentive to maintain the value of the loan sold (through monitoring covenants, for example) because future loans are going to be made. This explanation suggests that loan sales do not create any additional risk for the selling bank.

It is difficult to discern any regulatory implications from these results. If loan sales are feasible because banks implicitly offer put options, then to be consistent (if for no other reason), loan sales should be treated like other off–balance sheet items (i.e., perhaps subject to capital requirements). But, under the second explanation, no contingent liability is created and, consequently, there would be no regulatory implications.

REFERENCES

Bates, Philip S. (1986). "Back-Up Policies for Short-Term Notes." *Credit Week International* (April) (New York, Standard and Poor's).
Bennett, Barbara (1986). "Off–Balance Sheet Risk in Banking: The Case of Standby Letter of Credit." *Economic Review* (Winter) (Federal Reserve Bank of San Francisco), pp. 19–30.
Boyd, John, and Edward C. Prescott (1986). "Financial Intermediary-Coalitions." *Journal of Economic Theory* 38, pp. 211–232.
Calomiris, Charles W. (nd). "Comment on 'Commercial Paper, Bank Reserves, and the Informational Role of Loan Commitments.' " Northwestern University, mimeographed.
Diamond, Douglas W. (1984). "Financial Intermediation and Delegated Monitoring." *Review of Economic Studies* 51.
Flannery, Mark J. (1988). "Bank Risk Preferences with Deposit Insurance and Capital Regulation." University of North Carolina at Chapel Hill, mimeographed.
Gorton, Gary B., and Joseph G. Haubrich (1986). "Bank Deregulation, Credit Markets and the Control of Capital." *Carnegie-Rochester Conference Series on Public Policy* 26.
———. (1987). "Loan Sales, Recourse, and Reputation: An Analysis of Secondary Loan Participations." Rodney L. White Center for Financial Research Working Paper, The Wharton School, University of Pennsylvania.
Greenbaum, Stuart I., and Anjan V. Thakor (1987). "Bank Funding Modes: Securitization versus Deposits." *Journal of Banking and Finance* 11, pp. 379–402.
James, Christopher (1987a). "The Use of Loan Sales and Standby Letters of Credit by Commercial Banks." University of Oregon Working Paper.
———. (1987b). "Some Evidence on the Uniqueness of Bank Loans." *Journal of Financial Economics* 19(2), pp. 217–236.
Johnson, Herb, and Rene Stulz (1987). "The Pricing of Options with Default Risk." *Journal of Finance* 42(2), pp. 267–280.
Maddala, G. S. (1977). *Econometrics* (New York, McGraw-Hill).
Marcus, Alan J., and Israel Shaked (1984). "The Valuation of FDIC Deposit Insurance Using Option-Pricing Estimates." *Journal of Money, Credit, and Banking* 16(4) (November), pp. 446–460.
Melvin, Donald J. (1986). "A Primer for RMA Staff on Legal and Regulatory Concepts and Standards in the Securitization of Loans." (Philadelphia, Robert Morris Associates, mimeographed).
Merton, Robert C. (1974). "On the Pricing of Corporate Debt: The Risk Structure of Interest Rates." *Journal of Finance* 29, pp. 449–470.
———. (1977). "An Analytic Derivation of the Cost of Deposit Insurance and Loan Guarantees." *Journal of Banking and Finance* 1, pp. 3–11.

————. (1978). "On the Cost of Deposit Insurance When There Are Surveillance Costs." *Journal of Business* 51(3), pp. 439–476.

Pavel, Christine, and David Phillis (1987). "To Sell or Not to Sell: Loan Sales by Commercial Banks." Federal Reserve Bank of Chicago, mimeographed.

Pennacchi, George (1988). "Loan Sales and the Cost of Bank Capital." *Journal of Finance* 43, pp. 375–396.

Wolkowitz, Benjamin, et al. (1982). "Below the Bottom Line: The Use of Contingencies and Commitments by Commercial Banks." Staff Studies, Board of Governors of the Federal Reserve System.

Money Demand and Off–Balance Sheet Liquidity: Empirical Analysis and Implications for Monetary Policy

REUVEN GLICK* AND STEVEN E. PLAUT**

In recent years, off–balance sheet credit facilities have grown dramatically and now represent the most prevalent contractual framework within which commercial and industrial borrowing from banks occurs. One important role of these facilities is to provide liquidity to bank customers that acts as a substitute for on–balance sheet liquidity or "money."

This paper discusses empirical evidence of the substitutability between on– and off–balance sheet liquidity for the business sector. It also discusses the implications of this relationship for interest rate determination and monetary policy. In particular, it is argued that monetary policy should pay more attention to off–balance sheet liquidity when choosing targets and operating procedures.

I. Introduction

In recent years, off–balance sheet credit facilities provided by banks have been one of the most rapidly growing financial instruments both within the United States and overseas. Loans "under commitment" account for 79 percent of American commercial and industrial loans, 80 percent of construction and land development loans, and 60 percent of farm loans.[1] Continuing credit facilities in the form of credit cards and lines of credit are important sources of funds for consumer loans as well. Investment banks and brokerage houses also offer credit to customers under arrangements somewhat like commercial bank credit facilities.

The increasing role of credit facilities has important implications for the

*Federal Reserve Bank of San Francisco.

**School of Business, University of California at Berkeley.

The development of the paper benefited greatly from comments by Mark Flannery, John Judd, Arie Melnik, Brian Motley, Bharat Trehan, and Paul Wachtel. The opinions expressed herein are those of the authors and do not necessarily reflect the views of the Federal Reserve Bank of San Francisco or the Board of Governors of The Federal Reserve System.

1. *Federal Reserve Bulletin*, January 1988.

structure of credit markets, the stability and risk exposure of financial institutions, and the operation of monetary policy. Until recently, most of the research on credit facilities has concentrated on issues of pricing and contract structure. Recent contributions include Campbell (1978), Thakor, Hong, and Greenbaum (1981), Melnik and Plaut (1986), and Ham and Melnik (1987). Yet an important role of private-sector credit facilities that has received less attention is the provision of liquidity, supplementing "ordinary" transactions account balances held by households and firms at banks and other depository institutions. They provide funds on short or no notice that can be used to finance transactions, generally as conveniently as writing checks or using cash.

This paper empirically explores the interrelationship between on– and off–balance sheet liquidity. In particular, it examines "money demand" in the presence of off–balance sheet liquidity taking the form of unused loan commitments. By analyzing the degree of substitutability among these different forms of liquidity, we attempt to shed more light on the channels through which monetary policy operates.

Off–balance sheet credit facilities generally have several characteristics in common. They establish maximum credit ceilings, which either may not be exceeded by the customer or may be exceeded only at substantial penalty. They are continuing medium-term or long-term arrangements, often extending over several years. They usually employ multiple pricing components, including an interest charge (often floating) and facility fees of one sort or another.[2]

Credit facilities can be seen as providing a number of services to bank customers. They may provide credit availability insurance; they may provide option-like hedging services by protecting customers against disadvantageous changes in the pricing of credit or in customers' credit ratings; they may reduce credit-related transactions costs. Finally, they provide liquidity by entitling the customer to utilize additional funds besides demand deposit balances in order to make transactions.[3] In this paper we focus on this last aspect of facilities. Because these various services are provided jointly within the credit facility, it may be impossible to distinguish among them. For example, if credit utilized under a facility is diminished, it may be because the customer's credit needs have declined, because interest rate changes

---

2. Facility fees are sometimes specified as a fixed amount, sometimes assessed on the total credit commitment, and at other times assessed on unutilized funds.

3. Technically, when funds are drawn under a credit line, they are credited to the customer's transactions account and are then used to complete transactions.

have motivated liability restructuring, or simply because the customer seeks to expand his liquidity by increasing his unused line of credit.

Off–balance sheet liquidity in the form of unused loan commitments may be regarded as providing bank customers with a stock of liquidity that is potentially a substitute for "money." The notion that off–balance sheet liquidity might be used as a substitute for on–balance sheet liquidity ("money") is appealing on both the theoretical and empirical levels. An individual may purchase merchandise using cash, checking account balances, overdraft facilities, credit cards, or personal lines of credit, all with more or less the same ease, convenience, and transaction costs. Similarly, a firm may purchase goods using cash, checking account balances, revolving credit facilities, or loan commitments, all with negligible differences in terms of convenience and transaction costs. Therefore, for an individual or firm, off–balance sheet facilities theoretically represent "stocks" of potential transaction-related purchasing power, exactly like money. An individual holding several credit cards, or an unused line of credit, would be expected to hold smaller balances in demand deposits than would a similar individual who did not have these sources of liquidity. Similarly, firms would decrease their demand for money when their holdings of off–balance sheet liquidity grow. The converse should also be true: Holding more funds in transactions accounts should mean lower demand for off–balance sheet liquidity.[4]

Much of the monetary literature in recent years has focused on how financial deregulation has affected the substitutability between $M1$ and other on–balance sheet items such as monetary market deposit accounts, passbook savings, and other forms of liquid savings.[5] We argue that the substitutability of $M1$ and off–balance sheet liquidity may be similarly important.

The total quantity of unused credit under off–balance sheet facilities is in fact about the same order of magnitude as $M1$ itself. In June 1987 the level of unused commercial and industrial $(C + I)$ commitments at the 110 banks surveyed by the Federal Reserve System represented 51 percent of $M1$. (This figure does not include $C + I$ lines of credit at other institutions or non–$C + I$ lines.)[6]

---

4. Of course, firm and individual decisions regarding holdings of on– and off–balance sheet liquidity are not made independently. Moreover, they are not necessarily made *simultaneously,* since purchasing off–balance sheet facilities involves recontracting. (Typically, one alters his checking account balance more often than he does the number of his credit cards.) Hence, adjustments in on–balance sheet liquidity would be expected to occur more often, and faster, if taken in aggregate.

5. See Simpson and Porter (1980) and Judd and Trehan (1987).

6. The loan commitment data were provided by the Federal Reserve Board's Banking Studies Section. These data, which are no longer collected, were published in Federal Reserve Board Statistical Release G.21. Monthly figures are available for July 1973 through June 1987 only.

Although data are available for the off–balance sheet liquidity maintained by businesses (in the form of unused $C + I$ credit lines), comparable
data for the household sector are not. We therefore concentrate here primarily
on the business sector and, in particular, on the degree of substitution
between business-held off–balance sheet liquidity and on–balance sheet liquidity in the form of gross business demand deposits.[7]

For the period 1974Q1 through 1987Q2, the simple correlation coefficient between percentage quarterly changes in unused $C + I$ commitments
and in gross business demand deposits was -0.12. When business holdings
of demand deposits rise (fall), unused business credit lines tend to be adjusted
downward (upward).

Business holdings constitute the bulk of all gross demand deposit holdings. Although these are available on a quarterly basis only, total $M1$ is
available monthly. The simple correlation coefficient between percentage
monthly changes in $M1$ (which includes nonbusiness holdings) and unused
$C + I$ commitments is -0.27 for the period 1976:1 through 1987:6, and
-0.34 for the period 1979:1 through 1987:6. This casual analysis supports
the notion that money and loan commitments may serve as substitute forms
of liquidity.

The substitutability between money and off–balance sheet liquidity has
important implications for the transmission channels of monetary policy. In
recent years, attention has refocused on the issue of how monetary changes
are transmitted to the real sector. The traditional view was that money is
held primarily due to its usefulness and efficiency in conducting transactions
and that changes in money aggregates influence real economic activity
through the interest rate channel by affecting the opportunity cost of funds.
Such an approach may be traced back at least to Baumol (1952) and Tobin
(1956).

More recently, the monetary literature has attempted to connect off–
balance sheet credit facilities with monetary policy through the phenomenon
of credit availability and rationing. The credit rationing literature has grown
following Jaffee and Modigliani (1969), Jaffee and Russell (1976), and
Stiglitz and Weiss (1981). As noted by Melnik and Plaut (1986), the most
common institutional form for such rationing is the loan commitment contract. Blinder (1981) and Blinder and Stiglitz (1983) have theoretically
addressed the question of the operation of monetary policy under credit

---

7. The gross demand deposit data are published in Table 1.31 of the *Federal Reserve Bulletin*.
The raw data were available only in seasonally unadjusted form and were seasonally adjusted by taking
the residuals from a regression with seasonal linear dummies.

rationing. They have shown that in a rationing equilibrium, monetary policy has little if any effect on real activity through interest rate changes, but does have an effect through its impact on credit availability.

On the empirical side, a number of papers have attempted to determine whether credit quantity variables have real effects. Friedman (1982, 1983) has argued that total (net) credit is more closely related to real economic activity than narrower measures of liquidity, as measured by the various monetary aggregates. However, King (1986) and Bernanke (1986) have found little evidence that bank loans have predictive power for real economic activity or that banks ration loans.[8] Wojnilower (1985) and Sofianos, Wachtel, and Melnik (1987) have argued that the growth of off–balance sheet liquidity may explain the weakness of the credit rationing channel. In particular, Sofianos et al. empirically analyze the relation of credit utilized under loan commitments with monetary policy and real economic activity. They argue that loan contracts provide bank customers with a kind of insurance against credit rationing, and hence affect monetary policy by eliminating the quantity availability effects for these borrowers. They find evidence that money supply changes affect the volume of loans under commitment.

The existence of an interrelationship between on– and off–balance sheet liquidity has a number of important implications. First, the traditional view that short-term interest rates are determined by supply and demand for on–balance sheet monetary aggregates may be incorrect if off–balance sheet facilities represent a nonnegligible alternative source of liquidity. Second, the channels through which monetary policy operates are considerably more complex when both "types" of liquidity coexist. Open-market expansions or contractions of on–balance sheet liquidity may trigger adjustments in off–balance sheet liquidity. Interest rates and prices will then have to clear "both" liquidity markets, resulting in equilibria seemingly at odds with money demand analysis. Third, since off–balance sheet liquidity (in the form of unused loan commitments) is created through private-sector contracting between financial institutions and their customers, the total stock of liquidity (on and off the balance sheet) may be essentially beyond the control of the monetary authorities. An attempt to alter liquidity through open market operations may lead to countervailing adjustments in off–balance sheet liquidity. The latter may be expanded or contracted by private-

---

8. The evidence provided by Bernanke is actually mixed. Using vector autoregression (VAR) techniques, he finds no support for the existence of credit rationing. However, using a mixed VAR-structural approach, he finds evidence that credit flows may influence real activity as strongly as monetary aggregates.

sector agents in order to counter the on–balance sheet effects of monetary policy.[9]

The plan of the paper is as follows. In Section II we investigate the effects of off–balance sheet liquidity in the form of unused loan commitments within a conventional money demand equation. In Section III we discuss the implications of our analysis for monetary policy. Finally, in Section IV we discuss conclusions.

II. Money Demand in the Presence of Off–Balance Sheet Liquidity

Traditionally, money demand analysis has dealt with on–balance sheet liquidity separately from off–balance sheet liquidity. If, however, the two forms of liquidity are substitutes or if interest rates depend on total "liquidity demand," then analyzing money demand separately from off–balance sheet liquidity demand will lead to an incorrect representation of the interest rate determination process as well as misleading guidelines for monetary policy.

To shed some light on the interrelationship between on– and off–balance sheet liquidity, we investigate the effects of including loan commitments in a conventional money demand equation by adapting the error-correction specification approach of Hendry (1980). This specification is employed to take account of the lagged adjustment of private demand for money to changes in macroeconomic variables that determine this demand.[10] More specifically, we posit the following long-run relationship between money and its determinants:

$$log\ M_t = a_0 + a_1 log\ Y_t + a_2 R_t + a_3 log\ UC_t + e_t. \qquad (1)$$

Here M is the monetary aggregate, Y is an income scale variable, R is a short-term money market rate, UC is unused loan commitments, e is an error term representing the extent to which the public's actual money stock diverges from its equilibrium level, and t is a time subscript.

The short-run adjustment of money demand in a given period is assumed to depend on the divergence between its actual and equilibrium level at the beginning of the period, e_{t-1}, and on current (and possibly lagged) changes in the explanatory variables:

---

9. See Glick and Plaut (1988), a theoretical companion paper. There it is argued that monetary authorities lose control of interest rates and real variables due to such countervailing adjustment.

10. An advantage of the Hendry specification is that it does not require the long sample period needed for the estimation of explicit distributed lags, and it implies fewer restrictions on the response of money to its determinants than the partial adjustment model. It also allows the short-run impacts of changes in macroeconomic variables to differ from their long-run effects. For an application of this specification see Motley (1988).

$$\Delta logM_t = b_0 - b_1 e_{t-1} + \sum_p \Delta b_{2p} logM_{t-p} + \sum_q b_{3q} \Delta logY_{t-q}$$
$$+ \sum_s b_{4s} \Delta R_{t-s} + \sum_v b_{5v} \Delta logUC_{t-v}, \tag{2}$$

where Δ denotes the first difference operator.

Substituting (1) into (2) gives:

$$\Delta logM_t = b_0 + \sum_p b_{2p} \Delta logM_{t-p} + \sum_q b_{3q} \Delta logY_{t-q}$$
$$+ \sum_s b_{4s} \Delta R_{t-s} + \sum_v b_{5v} \Delta logUC_{t-v} \tag{3}$$
$$- b_1 \left(logM_{t-1} - a_0 - a_1 logY_{t-1} \right.$$
$$\left. - a_2 R_{t-1} - a_3 logUC_{t-1} \right).$$

In this equation a_1 represents the long-run income elasticity of demand for money; and a_2 multiplied by the level of R is the long-run interest elasticity. As the stock of money approaches its long-run equilibrium level more quickly, the larger are the coefficients on the lagged level of money (b_1) and the smaller are those on the changes in money, income, and the interest rate (b_{2p}, b_{3q}, and b_{4s}, respectively). The coefficient a_3 may be interpreted as the long-run substitutability of loan commitment liquidity for on–balance sheet liquidity (or M).

We estimated equation (3) using quarterly data for the period 1974Q1–1987Q2. Since the off–balance sheet data are available for the business sector only, we restrict the analysis to gross deposit holdings by the business sector. The other explanatory variables are defined in the usual way. Y is measured by nominal GNP, R by the three-month Treasury bill rate, and UC by total unused commercial and industrial loan commitments, as reported by the sample of large U.S. banks in the Monthly Survey of Commercial and Industrial Loan Commitments. Three dummy shift variables are used to remove outlying observations—one for a period of sharp increase in loan commitment usage in 1975Q1, a second for the "credit crunch" period 1980Q2, and a third for a short period of unusually large monetary growth, 1986Q4. Seasonal adjustment dummies are also included.

Representative results are reported in column 1 of Table 1. Observe that *changes* in income, unused loan commitments, and (lagged) money are all statistically nonsignificant, whereas the lagged change in the interest rate *is* significant. However, the lagged *levels* of these variables, representing the long-run determinants of money demand, are all significant except for the

TABLE 1

OLS Regression Estimates, 1974Q1–1987Q2

Dependent Variable	(1) $\Delta \log M_t$	(2) $\Delta \log UC_t$
Constant	1.78	.208
	(2.78)***	(.266)
$\Delta \log M_t$	−.007	−.193
	(−.048)	(−1.08)
$\Delta \log Y_t$	.397	.606
	(1.52)	(1.90)*
ΔR_t	.002	.004
	(1.02)	(1.27)
ΔR_{t-1}	.004	.001
	(−1.83)*	(.289)
$\Delta \log UC_{t-1}$	.032	.386
	(.358)	(3.48)***
$\log M_{t-1}$	−.293	−.102
	(−3.28)***	(−.933)
$\log Y_{t-1}$	.305	.206
	(3.73)***	(2.06)**
$\log R_{t-1}$	−.001	.005
	(−1.23)	(3.56)***
$\log UC_{t-1}$	−.120	−.124
	(−3.37)***	(−2.84)***
R^2	.95	.77
SEE	.015	.019
DW	2.05	2.22

Note: t-statistics are given in parentheses below coefficients, with statistics significant at the .10, .05, and .01 significance levels indicated by *, **, and *** respectively. Coefficients for dummy and seasonal variables are not reported.

interest rate. As expected, changes in current money demand depend positively on income and negatively on the interest rate and lagged money holdings. Most importantly for our purposes, money demand depends *negatively* on the level of unused loan commitments (*UC*). An increase in the level of unused loan commitments leads to a fall in money demand.

Although *UC* is an important explanatory variable for money demand, the converse was not the case. Column 2 in Table 1 reports the results of estimating an equation for the demand for unused off–balance sheet liquidity, analogous to Column 1. We observe that neither changes nor levels of money seem to affect the demand for unused loan commitment facilities.[11] Interestingly, the sign of the coefficient of the interest rate in the demand for off–balance sheet liquidity is opposite that for money demand. When the interest rate rises, businesses demand less money but *more* off–balance sheet liquidity. This may be so because they substitute the latter for on–balance

---

11. This may reflect the fact that recontracting to alter *UC* occurs infrequently.

FIGURE 1

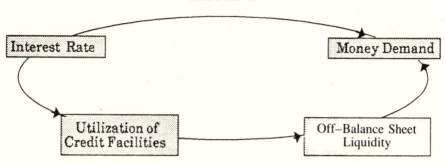

sheet liquidity, the holdings of which drop due to increases in opportunity costs. Similarly, it may be due to the fact that utilization of credit under these lines decreases, leaving greater unused liquidity. As we have seen, a change in off–balance sheet liquidity subsequently causes changes in *M*.

A major implication that may be drawn from the above results seems to be that changes in interest rates feed into the components of liquidity demand through different channels. A rise (fall) in the interest rate lowers (raises) demand for *M* and raises (lowers) demand for *UC*. Changes in *UC*, in turn, have a further effect on *M*, by causing *M* to be substituted for *UC*. The two effects on *M* work in opposite directions (Figure 1).[12]

III. The Implications for Monetary Policy

Under current regulations, off–balance sheet liquidity in the form of revolving credit facilities, lines of credit, and loan commitments represents a largely unregulated source of liquidity. These facilities are generally exempt from regulatory costs imposed on banks through reserve requirements, liquidity ratios, and so forth.[13] Banks and their customers may fully expand or contract the quantity of this form of liquidity on the basis of their own needs and costs.

The existence of off–balance sheet liquidity may influence the effectiveness of traditional monetary policy. When monetary policy produces expansion or contraction of on–balance sheet liquidity (or "money"), pri-

---

12. The results in this section are illustrative. A more-refined technique should try to estimate simultaneously the demand for money and off–balance sheet liquidity.

13. New capital requirements for off–balance sheet items are currently being implemented in the United States and several other countries.

FIGURE 2

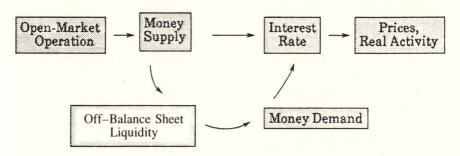

vate-sector agents may choose to offset this change to some extent through adjustments in their off–balance sheet liquidity "holdings." They may do so through altering the extent to which credit is utilized under existing lines of credit, raising or lowering the unused portion of the commitment. In addition, they may alter their off–balance sheet liquidity through recontracting, purchasing new lines, or canceling old lines.[14]

Thus, for example, an open-market operation involving the sale (purchase) of securities by the monetary authorities would initially contract (expand) liquidity and increase (decrease) the supply of bonds. If the private sector subsequently increased (decreased) its off–balance sheet liquidity through reducing (increasing) credit utilized under commitments, then the impact of the open-market operation on interest rates and real sector is unclear (Figure 2). If interest rates are determined by the aggregate supply and demand for "credit," then the open-market operation and the off–balance sheet adjustment response work in opposing directions, resulting in a small (or even ambiguous) *net* shift in credit demand. Similarly, the *net* stock of liquidity would decline by less than the change in "money," which might cushion the impact of open-market operations on interest rates and real activity. In a sense, monetary policy would become less effective.[15]

Another aspect of the role of off–balance sheet facilities in monetary policy relates to the proper aggregate to be targeted. Traditionally, $M1$ was considered to be the appropriate aggregate for money targeting, in the sense that it measured the quantity of the medium of payment and was thought

---

14. Because contracting for facilities occurs infrequently, adjustments in off–balance sheet liquidity may occur slowly. Hence, the monetary implications of off–balance sheet liquidity are likely to be different in the long and short run. This indeed is supported by the findings in the above empirical section, where lagged unused commitment levels and anticipated future adjustments therein seem to affect money demand.

15. See Glick and Plaut (1988).

to be the aggregate most closely correlated with prices and real activity. In recent years $M1$ has been increasingly abandoned, both by researchers and by policymakers. Monetarists today often speak of $M2$ or some broader monetary aggregate as their recommended target. The Federal Reserve System currently focuses more on $M2$ and $M3$ (to the extent that it targets any monetary aggregate) rather than on $M1$.

The abandonment of $M1$ seems to have been motivated by the fact that $M1$ velocity has shifted excessively in recent years. Over the same period, quasi-money aggregates have expanded rapidly and the $M1$-based money demand equations have seemed to lose much of their predictive powers and some of their econometric fit.[16] However, off–balance sheet liquidity also grew rapidly over this period. Financial innovation related to these facilities probably occurred as quickly as it did for the nontransactions account components of $M2$ and $M3$. It remains for future empirical research to determine whether a "liquidity" measurement, consisting of $M1$ plus off–balance sheet unused facilities, performs better than $M2$ or $M3$ in terms of explaining market equilibriums and as a guideline or target for monetary policy. In any case, $M2$ and $M3$ may reflect substitution away from $M1$, but so again may off–balance sheet facilities.

Finally, there seems to have occurred in recent decades a general increase in the volatility of interest rates. Certainly the 1970s and 1980s have been "noisier" than the 1950s and 1960s. Some have interpreted this as a symptom of a general loss in monetary control by central banks. It may be that the "noise" stems from the rapid growth in off–balance sheet liquidity, reducing the correlation between $M1$ and total liquidity. We know of no evidence that monetary authorities have looked at unused commitments when formulating policy or that they have targeted total liquidity or even considered it as a relevant factor. Our analysis suggests that such an experiment should be considered.

IV. Conclusions and Summary

The debates over monetary policy and monetary targeting have been largely restricted to forms of liquidity appearing on the balance sheets of financial institutions. Much of the debate has been over which liabilities of these institutions should be properly counted as "money," and hence which are thought to represent the appropriate target for monetary policy.

Interestingly, little attention has been paid to the monetary importance of contingent liabilities of these institutions in the form of off–balance sheet

---

16. See Simpson and Porter (1980) and Judd and Scadding (1982).

credit facilities. These facilities provide a medium of exchange capacity and represent a liquidity substitute for on–balance sheet "money."

We have presented empirical evidence consistent with this view. Unused commitments appear to be a significant argument in money demand functions. Firms and individuals appear to jointly determine their demand for on–balance sheet and off–balance sheet liquidity, where one may be substituted for the other.

This has a number of important implications for interest rate determination and monetary policy. To the extent that interest rate adjustment ultimately clears a "liquidity" market, the substitutability of on– and off–balance sheet aggregates weakens the relationship between money, interest rates, and other variables of concern to policymakers.

If this view is correct, monetary authorities should be targeting, or at least watching, *total* liquidity, including unused off–balance sheet credit facilities. Short-term discretionary control of this aggregate may prove quite difficult, however, given the tendency of off–balance sheet liquidity to countervail changes in "money," including those generated by monetary "surprises" or unanticipated shocks in monetary policy.

Finally, it may be desirable to address the issue of regulation of off–balance sheet liquidity. Similar debates for on–balance sheet money and bank liabilities often involve trade-offs between macro and micro considerations. The former include arguments for regulation to improve monetary control and prevent macroeconomic instability. Micro considerations might dictate opposition to more regulation in order to achieve efficiency in banking operations and credit allocation. Off–balance sheet liquidity or contingent liabilities for financial institutions have been much less regulated than on–balance sheet activities. Any changes in this state must be weighed in light of the same sorts of micro and macro considerations.

REFERENCES

Baumol, William. "The Transaction Demand for Cash—An Inventory Theoretic Approach." *Quarterly Journal of Economics* 66, 1952, pp. 545–556.

Bernanke, B. "Alternative Explanations of the Money-Income Correlation." *Carnegie-Rochester Conference Series on Public Policy,* no. 25, Autumn 1986, pp. 49–100.

Blinder, Alan. "Credit Rationing and Effective Supply Failures." *Economic Journal* 97, June 1987, pp. 327–352.

Blinder, Alan, and Joseph Stiglitz. "Money, Credit Constraints, and Economic Activity." *American Economic Review* 73, May 1983, pp. 297–302.

Campbell, T. "A Model of the Market for Lines of Credit." *Journal of Finance* 33, 1978, pp. 231–44.

Friedman, Benjamin M. "Using a Credit Aggregate Target to Implement Monetary Policy in the Financial Environment of the Future." *Monetary Policy Issues in the 1980s.* Federal Reserve Bank of Kansas City, 1982.

———. "Monetary Policy with a Credit Aggregate Target." *Carnegie-Rochester Conference Series on Public Policy,* no. 18, 1983, pp. 117–148.

Glick, Reuven, and Steven Plaut. "Off-Balance-Sheet Liquidity and Monetary Control." Manuscript, February 1988.

Hakkio, Craig, and Charles Morris. "Vector Autoregressions: A User's Guide." Federal Reserve Bank of Kansas City, Working Paper 84-10, November 1984.

Ham, John C., and Arie Melnik. "Loan Demand: An Empirical Analysis Using Micro Data." *Review of Economics and Statistics* 69, November 1987, pp. 704–709.

Hendry, David. "Predictive Failure and Econometric Modelling in Macroeconomics: The Transaction Demand for Money." In P. Omerod (ed.), *Economic Modelling*. London, 1979.

Jaffee, Dwight, and Franco Modigliani. "A Theory and Test of Credit Rationing." *American Economic Review* 65, December 1969, pp. 850–872.

Jaffee, Dwight, and Thomas Russell. "Imperfect Information, Uncertainty, and Credit Rationing." *Quarterly Journal of Economics* 90, November 1976, pp. 651–666.

Judd, John, and John Scadding. "The Search for a Stable Money Demand Function: A Review of the Post-1973 Literature." *Journal of Economic Literature* 20, 1982, pp. 994–1023.

Judd, John, and Bharat Trehan. "Portfolio Substitution and the Reliability of M1, M2 and M3 as Monetary Policy Indicators." *Economic Review*. Federal Reserve Bank of San Francisco, Summer 1987.

King, Stephen. "Monetary Transmission: Through Bank Loans or Bank Liabilities?" *Journal of Money, Credit, and Banking* 28, August 1986, pp. 290–303.

Melnik, Arie, and Steven E. Plaut. "Loan Commitment Contracts, Terms of Lending and Credit Allocation." *Journal of Finance* 41, June 1986, pp. 425–435.

Motley, Brian. "Should M2 Be Redefined?" *Economic Review*. Federal Reserve Bank of San Francisco, Winter 1988, pp. 33–51.

Santomero, Anthony. "The Role of Transaction Costs and Rates of Return on the Demand Deposit Decision." *Journal of Monetary Economics* 5, 1979, pp. 343–364.

Simpson, Thomas, and Richard Porter. "Some Issues involving the Definition and Interpretation of Monetary Aggregates." In *Controlling Monetary Aggregates III*. Federal Reserve Bank of Boston, Conference Series No. 23, 1980, pp. 161–234.

Sims, Christopher. "Macroeconomics and Reality." *Econometrica* 48, January 1980, pp. 1–48.

Sofianos, G., P. Wachtel, and A. Melnick. "Loan Commitments and Monetary Policy." NBER Working Paper No. 2232, May 1987.

Stiglitz, J., and A. Weiss. "Credit Rationing in Markets with Imperfect Information." *American Economic Review* 71, June 1981, pp. 393–410.

Thakor, Anjan, Hai Hong, and Stuart I. Greenbaum. "Bank Loan Commitments and Interest Rate Volatility." *Journal of Banking and Finance* 5, 1981, pp. 497–510.

Tobin, James. "The Interest Elasticity of Transactions Demand for Cash." *Review of Economics and Statistics* 84, 1956, pp. 241–247.

Wojnilower, Albert M. "Private Credit Demand, Supply, and Crunches—How Different Are the 1980s?" *AEA Papers and Proceedings* 75, May 1985, pp. 351–356.

Discussion of Off–Balance Sheet Activities: Banking and Monetary Policy

MARK J. FLANNERY*

The financial and economic dimensions of banks' off–balance sheet (OBS) activities involve important and interesting issues for bankers, regulators, and academics. Many of the financial products we are discussing here today occupy a point at the intersection of ''intermediated'' and ''open-market'' financial services and problems. Therefore, these papers necessarily raise questions about the basic functioning of intermediary firms, and the value they add to the economy. And since we regulate banking firms so much more intensively than we regulate open-market securities transactions, it is no surprise that OBS activities pose some difficult problems for the regulatory structure we have built up over the past fifty-five years.

It seems to me that OBS banking raises the following questions which economic analysis can help address:

1. What private incentives have lead *banks* to engage in OBS activities at such a prodigious rate over the past five to seven years?
2. How are *borrowers* affected by the factors that have caused this relatively substantial rearrangement in the way capital markets channel loanable funds from ultimate lenders to ultimate borrowers?
3. How does the recent trend toward OBS banking affect the *riskiness* of individual banks? Of the banking system? Of the deposit insurance funds?
4. What are the *macroeconomic* implications of these capital market rearrangements?

The papers we have heard this morning address various aspects of all of these questions, though they have least to say (as a group) about the regulatory implications at a micro level.

This is a notable omission from such a group of papers, though it is not a serious indictment of any one. As several of the papers have argued, there are likely to be alternative reasons for the recent explosion of OBS bank activities. However, I strongly believe that one very important factor in

---

*University of North Carolina at Chapel Hill

many of these decisions is what Ed Kane calls "structural arbitrage," whereby firms seek to provide services in a form that draws the least amount of regulatory interference. It is accordingly very important to relate the other questions I have identified above to the current and proposed regulatory structure.

I turn now to the individual papers.

James

The paper by James takes us to the micro level by providing one indication of why securitizing loans would be profitable for banking firms. James' argument is that loan sales are equivalent to an SLC, and to debt securitized by specific bank assets. Because bankers are generally not allowed to securitize their deposits, they resort to loan sales as a means of achieving the same ends. In particular, securitizing debt reduces the extent of Myers' (1977) underinvestment bias for a levered firm with risky debt. Only by segmenting the cash flows associated with new, low-risk assets can bankers earn rents on new loan projects that come to them in imperfect loan markets. The equivalence of loan sales and secured debt is insightful and explains loan securitization without relying on capital adequacy regulation.

As James points out, loan sales could be driven by a variety of factors, so his explanation here does not necessarily compete with others, which focus more explicitly on bankers' regulatory restrictions. In fact, the use of loan sales by unregulated entities such as Ford Motor Credit implies that there is more going on here than regulatory avoidance. However, note that the bank's use of loan sales is optimal only because explicit securitization is not permitted under current regulations. In other words, we still have no explanation for loan sales that is entirely free of regulatory influence.

Another question suggested by James' analysis is how bankers (and their customers) choose between loan sales and SLC. Since both have the same impact on bank profitability, the analysis here says nothing about how to choose between them. In this way, James' conclusion feeds into Gorton and Pennacchi's (GPI) basic question: How can intermediated assets be sold to the open market? Combining James and GP1, it appears that loans sales might well be viewed as a *composite product* in which the banker earns a return on underwriting services and also provides an implicit SLC. To evaluate this possibility, we would need data on the margins banks earn on loan sales, compared with what they charge for an SLC for similar customers issuing commercial paper.

Finally, the model presented here explicitly assumes that bank depositors are not fully insured. (This is an important empirical question, about which I have some very preliminary evidence suggesting that bank CD rates do contain measurable risk premia.) James explains that complete *de facto* insurance would remove the underinvestment problem entirely. Banks might still originate low-risk loans for resale, but they would not wish to finance them in their own portfolio. Flannery (1988) discusses this incentive.

In sum, the James paper brings good finance analysis to bear on the question of why loan sales are profitable for the banks involved. In combination with explanations based on capital adequacy regulation, this insight adds to our understanding of the private incentives to engage in this type of OBS activities.

Gorton and Pennacchi

Gorton and Pennacchi's (GP1) paper addresses the question of what value is added by the process of loan securitization, though from a partial equilibrium perspective. They eschew explicit consideration of the reason a bank chooses to sell loans,[1] but they ask whether the selling bank is providing credit-guarantee services in the process of securitization. The authors first synthesize a set of "stylized facts" about the loan sale market and place these facts in a useful conceptual framework. They then undertake an econometric estimation that is both clever and brave.

GP1's paper is primarily motivated by the observation that intermediated assets differ fundamentally from securities that are sold in the open market. In particular, bank assets are originated by banks because they have some sort of comparative advantage (over other market participants) in originating or monitoring that particular type of credit arrangement. They then point out that the idea of selling such specialized loans to other parties is potentially at odds with the notion that banks provide valuable financial services.

How, then, can the idea of bank value added be combined with the observation that some loans are sold to third parties? GP1 offer two possibilities.

1. Securitized loans are not really intermediated securities, but are commercial paper in disguise. Banks' loan sales represent simple underwriting services, by which commercial bankers compete with investment bankers within the confines of Glass Steagall. It seems clear that there is a sizable element of truth to this assessment. (For example, their Table 1 indicates that the average rate on sold loans is twenty-seven to forty basis points below the rate on comparably rated commercial paper. This observation is

1. One of the authors (Pennacchi [1988]) has previously compared loan sales and additional deposits as alternative ways of providing loan customers with credit.

consistent with the hypothesis that bankers sell only the highest-quality paper in each rating category.) But GP1 argue that this cannot be the whole story because the available (sketchy) data indicate that one-third of 1985 loan sales involved loans "to companies that did not have access to the commercial paper market."

How, then, can other parties economically purchase these loans from bankers who possess significantly superior information about credit quality? First of all, note that bankers have done precisely this in the form of loan participations for many years. GP1 point out that recent loan sales have involved nonbank buyers, but we do not know that loan sellers are not selling *de facto* commercial paper to their nonbank customers, and selling loans that have traditionally been participated to other banks. However, GP1 offer another explanation.

2. They observe that bankers may offer implicit put options (or some other form of guarantee) on the sold loans. These guarantees cannot be explicit if the bank is to avoid holding capital, but the price at which loans are sold will reflect the buyer's assessment of what guarantees are being extended by the selling bank.

Having observed that there is one *possible* way that loan sales could constitute more than simply a restricted form of underwriting activity, GP1 take the only available source of data on loan sales—which is rather ill-suited to the task at hand—and proceed to estimate whether the sold loans are priced to reflect an implied bank guarantee. Their finding that loan sale spreads are significantly related to the perceived risk of selling banks is striking, especially considering their data's substantial errors in variable problems and the small number of observations.

I found this empirical work clever and intriguing. In particular, GP1 have employed a set of assumptions and transformations that allow them to extract the maximum possible information out of a small data set. However, their evidence did not *convince* me that banks must in fact be offering implied guarantees. Their results are certainly consistent with this possibility (especially in light of their discussion of vulnerable American puts), but there are other plausible interpretations. For example:

1. GP1's bank risk premium is essentially driven by changes in the bank stock price.
2. Bank stock prices tend to fall when market interest rates rise, which thus tends to increase the bank risk premium (b_t).
3. LIBOR is a risky rate, whose spread over a truly riskless rate will tend to vary with the level of market rates (see Merton [1974]).
4. Therefore, a change in riskless interest rates can simultaneously

influence both the bank risk premium and the yield spread, whose correlations are reported in Tables 2 and 3. Although I have no evidence that this is in fact the reason for GP1's significant correlations, the fact that there is a plausible alternative to their explanation is important in evaluating the implications of the empirical findings.

GP1's empirical work represents a useful and intriguing start. It could be improved with two relatively easy changes. First, rather than going "around the block" to impute CD risk premia from stock prices, the authors could collect a relatively small number of actual CD rates. Though I am unaware of any existing data source, the number of observations required does not preclude a direct appeal to the three banks involved (or to a dealer in bank CDs).

Second, though their exposition deals with risk premia over a riskless interest rate, GP1 use LIBOR in place of the riskless rate. LIBOR is a risky rate whose premium may well change with the same factors that affect their constructed variable b_t. It seems they should use a Treasury rate instead, or at least as an alternative.

GP1 conclude their paper with a brief discussion of their findings' implications for capital adequacy regulation. They argue quite reasonably that if bankers are extending implicit guarantees, their volume of sold loans should not be removed completely from their balance sheets.

Glick and Plaut

Glick and Plaut (GP2) take a macroeconomic and regulatory view by evaluating whether one type of OBS product—unused C&I credit lines—is likely to have a detrimental effect on monetary policy. Their view (along the lines of "what do OBS activities do for the private parties involved?") is that credit rationing is an important (perhaps dominant) channel of monetary policy control. They indicate that prearranged credit lines allow firms to avoid the rationing effects of monetary policy changes, and therefore may weaken the impact of monetary policy on real economic activity. Implicitly, therefore, spot credit is qualitatively different from prearranged lines. Although this type of reasoning is implied in the first part of the paper, it is not spelled out fully enough to make interpretation of the ensuing empirical work easy.[2]

This view that the existence of close substitutes for narrowly defined money may influence monetary policy is not a new one. Keynes' *Treatise*

---

2. Their theoretical view is explained more fully in a companion paper by the same authors (1988).

on Money (1930) suggested that unused credit lines might well be included in a definition of money, and Hawtrey (1919) observed that "credit and money are both equally media of exchange."

More recently, researchers have investigated the impact of "near-monies" on the demand for the monetary aggregates (e.g., Lee [1966] or GP2's references to Judd and Scadding [1982] or Judd and Trehan [1987]). In fact, economists in the late 1860s and 1870s wrestled with the same problem, debating whether checking accounts should be included in the definition of money, or whether it was merely a means of economizing on true money—which at the time meant specie and currency.

The general expression that has been applied to such interrelationships is that they constitute "slippages" or "leakages" in the transmission of monetary policy. As long as the slippages are constant through time, the Fed will understand how to interpret its various aggregates and can determine the appropriate size for policy actions. Difficulties arise, however, when some poorly understood event causes nonmoney assets (or liabilities) to expand (contract) rapidly *relative to* measured money. In this circumstance, continued reliance on historical relationships can easily lead the Fed astray. In other words, private incentives to innovate substitutes for money balances might make the demand for money unstable, which is the primary argument against relying on a monetary aggregate as the Fed's only intermediate target.[3]

However, this is precisely where GP2 provide us with no real information. They enumerate four different reasons that nonfinancial firms demand formal credit lines, but only one is directly relevant to the balance of their paper. They treat all C&I credit lines as the corporate equivalent of consumer credit card lines, even though we have evidence that many of these unused lines are meant only as backing for commercial paper. Unfortunately, we have no basis for sorting out truly "spendable" credit lines from the others (for example, lines backing commercial paper issues), though there appears to be anecdotal evidence that the latter component is what has grown most substantially in recent years.

In order to see why different types of lines will have different macroeconomic effects, consider explicitly the fact that bankers must supply the liquidity associated with unused credit lines. Banks must rearrange their balance sheets to provide the liquidity that may be taken by customers against their unused lines. Since something like 70 percent of loans made under prior commitments carry a floating interest rate, any impact of these ag-

---

3. Poole (1970) describes the conditions under which the Fed would optimally target the money stock alone, interest rates alone, or a combination.

gregate bank financial decisions on market interest rates will be largely passed through to borrowing entities.

A line take-down requires the bank to do one of three things:

1. Reduce loans outstanding to another element of the private sector. This does not change private-sector liquidity, although unused lines do fall.
2. Reduce their holdings of government bonds. Such systematic sales will tend to raise interest rates and may thus be consistent with monetary policy objectives.
3. Issue additional liabilities to finance the new loan balances. If the new bank liabilities are added to an unchanged stock of nonfinancial paper outstanding, this expands nonfinancial firm "liquidity" and raises interest rates. However, if customers are using their credit lines to replace commercial paper, the macroeconomic effects are likely to be slim, though unused lines again fall.

In short, I wish GP2 had sketched out more fully how they think a change in unused credit lines will counteract the intended thrust of monetary policy. I also wish we had the data to indicate what *type* of credit lines have grown most prominently in recent years.

However, GP2 have reminded us of a very important possibility: that the recent explosion in OBS activities might have an important impact on macro-level variables, in addition to the more tangible effects on the individual firms involved.

REFERENCES

Diamond, Douglas. "Financial Intermediaries and Delegated Monitoring." *Review of Economic Studies* (July 1984), pp. 393–415.
Flannery, Mark J. "Bank Risk Preferences with Deposit Insurance and Capital Regulation." University of North Carolina at Chapel Hill, mimeograph, January 1988.
Glick, Reuven, and Steven Plaut. "Off-Balance-Sheet Liquidity and Monetary Control." Manuscript, February 1988.
Hawtrey, R.G. *Currency and Credit* (London: Longmans, Green, 1919).
Judd, John, and John Scadding. "The Search for a Stable Money Demand Function: A Review of the Post-1973 Literature." *Journal of Economic Literature* (1982), pp. 994–1023.
Judd, John, and Bharat Trehan. "Portfolio Substitution and the Reliability of M1, M2, and M3 as Monetary Policy Indicators." *Economic Review*, Federal Reserve Bank of San Francisco (Summer 1987).
Keynes, John Maynard. *Treatise on Money.* Vol. 1 (New York: Harcourt, Brace, 1930).
Lee, Tong Hun. "Substitutability of Non-Bank Intermediary Liabilities for Money: The Empirical Evidence." *Journal of Finance* (September 1966), pp. 441–458.
Merton, Robert C. "On the Pricing of Corporate Debt: The Risk Structure of Interest Rates." *Journal of Finance* (1974), pp. 449–470.
Myers, Stewart. "Determinants of Corporate Borrowing." *Journal of Financial Economics* (1977), pp. 147–175.

Pennacchi, George. "Loan Sales and the Cost of Bank Capital." *Journal of Finance,* June, 1988, pp. 375–396.

Poole, William. "Optimal Choice of Monetary Policy Instruments in a Simple Stochastic Macro Model." *Quarterly Journal of Economics* (May 1970), pp. 197–216.

Part II

Financial Reporting and Off–Balance Sheet Transactions

Joshua Ronen* and Ashwinpaul C. Sondhi**

Off-Balance Sheet (OBS) activities are invariably economic transactions and events with real current or future cash flow consequences. However, the resulting economic assets and/or liabilities do not meet existing accounting definitions and/or measurement standards and are not currently recognized as accounting assets or liabilities. Since all OBS activities involve, to some degree, transfers of interest rate risk, credit risk, or liquidity risk, their nonrecognition in financial statements makes it difficult to assess their impact on the risk and return chracteristics of investments in both financial and nonfinancial businesses.

The proliferation of OBS transactions raises questions about the appropriate regulatory response to and adequacy of accounting standards for these activities. Their impact on enterprise risk and valuation is a significant concern. The first series of papers addressed the motivation for the proliferation of OBS transactions among suppliers of capital, such as the banking system. The second set of papers deals with the role of the financial reporting system given OBS transactions, for example, does market rationality and efficiency depend on full disclosure of these activities? Are there sufficient incentives for these disclosures in the absence of accounting regulations? If accounting standards are necessary, how should they be structured?

The Financial Accounting Standards Board (FASB) has been deliberating those issues for quite some time. Robert Swieringa, a member of the FASB, details its efforts to address recognition and measurement of financial instruments based on the economic substance of the rights and obligations conveyed by these

*Research Professor of Accounting, New York University
**Associate Professor of Accounting, New York University

instruments. However, it is difficult to specify unambiguously the rights and obligations conveyed by those transactions since the resulting components may themselves be contingent upon the accounting treatment of those instruments either as completed sales or secured financing transactions. The author suggests that the identification of rights and obligations and the accounting treatment may be interdependent, further exacerbating the standard setting problem.

Some authors (see Stewart and Neuhausen [1986]) have suggested that previous attempts at developing accounting rules—such as the reporting of transfers of receivables—were excessively legal and emphasized the transfer of control. It is not clear that the FASB will be able to develop consistent, generalized recognition and measurement rules for the myriad financial instruments in existence. Extensive disclosure rules may provide the optimal base for resolving these issues.

The FASB's November 1987 Exposure Draft (ED [1987]) adopted this approach in proposing to require improved disclosure of exposure to various risk categories. Swieringa reports on the deliberations surrounding the issuance of this ED (1987) in an addendum included in this volume. In July 1989, the FASB issued an Exposure Draft (ED [1989]) proposing disclosure requirements for financial instruments with OBS risk and concentrations of credit risk for all financial instruments. The addendum also discusses the FASB's "building block" approach to recognition and measurement issues.

Donegan and Sunder suggest that the intertemporal stability of financial reporting standards requires the explicit consideration of game-theoretic behavior among economic agents as a response to accounting rules. The authors suggest that the FASB may not have been very rational in failing to attribute to the market sufficient rationality; for example, they stopped short of recognizing that market participants would engage in enlightened pursuit of self-interest. The response to lease accounting rules through changes in lease contracts constitutes a telling example of this problem.

The authors suggest that it will be difficult to develop accounting rules incorporating highly uncertain components of OBS transactions and yet continue to provide perfectly articulated financial statements. The statistical properties of OBS transactions are seen to imply probabilistic reporting or financial estimates; this inference appears to embody the disclosure rules proposed by the FASB.

Donegan and Sunder suggest that complex disclosure rules may provide the answer; a course implicit in Swieringa's depiction of the FASB's approch.

In contrast to the normative tenor of these two papers, the final papers constitute descriptive analyses of responses to accounting rules. El-Gazzar, Lilien, and Pastena analyze the use of operating lease accounting to mitigate the effects of binding covenant constraints. Debt contracts negotiated prior to 1976 by intensive lessees are analyzed.

The evidence suggests that covenants restricting dividends, additional debt, production and investment decisions, and the patterns of payoffs are based on Generally Accepted Accounting Principles (GAAP) accounting methods and shows insignificant tailoring of accounting methods to constrain management incentives to use OBS transactions. Thus, the FASB may have been justified in believing that at least some segments of the market may be acting as if they were irrational in that bondholders did not seem to explicitly adjust covenants for the existence of OBS leases.

The final paper evaluates another OBS activity, the creation of finance subsidiaries, which is broadly seen as an attempt to increase debt capacity through implicit obligations not reflected on the balance sheet. Ronen and Sondhi show that finance subsidiaries can be used to increase debt capacity if accompanied by appropriate guarantees by the parent of the assets and profitability of the subsidiary. These implicit guarantees may impose higher risk on stockholders coincident with higher returns due to increased financial leverage. Thus, the FASB seems to be justified in requiring the consolidation of the OBS debt of these finance subsidiaries. However, the authors show that even after consolidation, the implicit guarantees will not be fully disclosed and the value of the stockholders' obligation would not be fully reflected.

The paper details various explicit guarantees including parent guarantees of profitability and cash flows of the finance subsidiary, provisions for additional and continuing parent equity investment in the subsidiary, and stringent covenants designed to protect the investments of the lenders to the subsidiary. However, no evidence of the implicit guarantees suggested above was found. As Gorton and Pennacchi suggested with respect to the form of implicit guarantees on loans sales, it is possible that lenders to the subsidiary perceive parent guarantees to include the implicit guarantee to contribute required capital.

The FASB's 1989 ED proposing enhanced disclosure require-
ments, and its continuing Financial Instruments project with its
focus on recognition and measurement issues, reflect its continuing
efforts to develop relevant financial reporting requirements.

Recognition and Measurement Issues in Accounting for Securitized Assets

ROBERT J. SWIERINGA*

The development of securities backed by loans has created huge and increasingly liquid markets. Millions of loans that used to be reflected on the balance sheets of lending institutions have been converted into securities. Residential mortgage-backed securities, which were introduced in the early 1970s, still account for most of the securitized assets outstanding. Recently, other types of loans, including car loans, commercial mortgages, credit cards, lease receivables, and even insurance policy loans, have been securitized. The resulting securitized assets provide investors with standardized, liquid, and easily financed instruments in markets that formerly offered only nonstandard and illiquid loans (Bryan [1986, 1987, 1988]).

Securitized assets raise many accounting recognition and measurement issues (Stewart and Neuhausen [1986]). Some of those issues arise because the accounting implications of alternative ways of structuring transactions to securitize assets are not addressed in the accounting literature; others arise because the existing literature provides conflicting guidance when applied by analogy to new issues. Some transactions apparently have been structured to raise cash from loans that are under water (cost exceeds current market value) without recognizing a loss. Other transactions have been structured to move assets and liabilities off the balance sheet even though all risks and rewards were not transferred.

In May 1986, the Financial Accounting Standards Board (FASB) added a major project to its agenda to address financial instruments and off–balance sheet financing issues. One of those issues is when financial assets and liabilities should be removed from or should not appear on balance sheets. Transactions that are structured to securitize assets range from outright sales of financial assets or interests in those assets to borrowings collateralized by those assets. This paper briefly outlines the scope of the FASB project and then focuses on recognition and measurement issues that arise in accounting for transactions structured to securitize assets.

---

*Member, Financial Accounting Standards Board. Expressions of individual views by members of the FASB and its staff are encouraged. The views expressed in this paper are those of Mr. Swieringa. Official positions of the FASB on accounting matters are determined only after extensive due process and deliberation.

The Financial Instruments Project

The financial instruments project is expected to develop broad standards to aid in resolving existing financial accounting and reporting issues and other issues that will likely arise in the future about various financial instruments and transactions. The issues to be addressed in this project include the following:

1. Disclosures about financial instruments, both about items not recognized and about obligations, commitments, and guarantees not now recognized in balance sheets.
2. Derecognition, nonrecognition, and offsetting issues, including whether financial assets should be considered sold if there is recourse or other continuing involvement with them and whether financial liabilities should be considered settled when assets are dedicated to settle them.
3. How to account for financial instruments and transactions that seek to transfer market or credit risks, including hedges, options, commitments, nonrecourse arrangements, and guarantees.
4. How financial instruments should be measured, for example, at market value, original cost, or lower of cost or market.
5. How issuers should account for securities with both debt and equity characteristics.
6. What effect separate legal entities and trusts should have on recognition of financial instruments and transactions.

Exposure Draft about Disclosures

The FASB initially has focused on improving disclosures about recognized and unrecognized financial instruments. An Exposure Draft of a proposed Statement, *Disclosures about Financial Instruments,* was issued in November 1987 (FASB [1987b]). That proposed Statement would require the following disclosures about all financial instruments:

Credit risk—maximum credit risk, reasonably possible and probable credit risks, and concentrations of risk in individual counterparties or groups of counterparties engaged in similar activities or activities in the same region.

Future cash receipts and payments—amounts contracted to be received or paid within one year, after one year through five years, and after five years, and amounts denominated in foreign currencies if significant.

Interest rates—amounts of interest-bearing financial instruments contracted to reprice or mature within one year, after one year through five years, and after five years, and their effective interest rates, and amounts denominated in foreign currencies if significant.

Market values—determined by quoted market prices or estimated, unless the entity is unable to determine or estimate the market value.

The proposed disclosures are based on present practices, and some of the proposed requirements are already met by present financial reports, although other proposed requirements are new. The proposed Statement is intended to make disclosures about financial instruments more comprehensive and comparable. The FASB is working with several companies that have agreed to participate in a test application of the Exposure Draft. The objective of that test application is to obtain a better understanding of the feasibility of implementing the suggested disclosure requirements, the cost of implementation, and the usefulness of the resulting information. Analysis of that test application and of letters commenting on the Exposure Draft will help the FASB decide what changes may be needed and whether to issue a final Statement.

Recognition and Measurement

The FASB staff is now studying derecognition, nonrecognition, and offsetting issues; how to account for financial instruments and transactions that transfer market or credit risk; and how to measure financial instruments. The plan is to prepare a discussion document with the assistance of a task force. The FASB expects to conduct public hearings on that document and then to proceed to deliberations that are expected to lead to Exposure Drafts beginning in 1989 or 1990.

Accounting for Securitized Assets

Securitized assets are created by a large and diverse collection of carefully structured transactions and financial instruments. Figure 1 summarizes the sequence of events and relations among the parties in a typical creation of securitized assets.

A financial institution collects mortgage loans with similar characteristics in a pool and transfers the rights to the loans in that pool to a trust without recourse (except in the case of defective documentation) in exchange for cash and for subordinate rights to all or part of the residual cash flows upon termination of the trust. The trust sells senior and subordinate rights

FIGURE 1

Events and Relations for Securitized Assets

I. At Inception

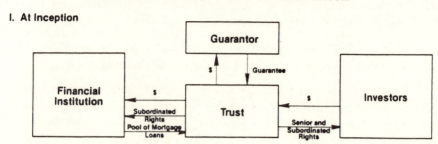

II. Collections

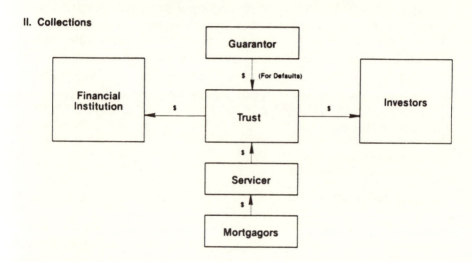

III. At Termination

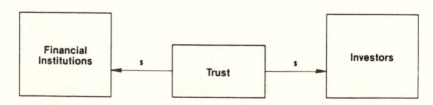

to the cash flows from the mortgage pool to investors in exchange for cash.
Those rights may be in the form of pass-through certificates that represent
individual undivided ownership interests in the cash flows from the mortgage
pool, or they may be in the form of debt obligations of the trust that are
secured by the pool of mortgage loans.

Those debt obligations can vary in the extent to which their cash flows are linked to the cash flows of the underlying mortgage loans. For example, some mortgage-backed bonds directly link their cash flows to those of the underlying mortgages. The cash flows from the mortgage pool may be paid out pro rata or may be prioritized among several different classes or tranches, resulting in a series of obligations with varying maturities. However, other mortgage-backed bonds do not link their cash flows to those of the underlying mortgages. If all cash received is not passed through to investors, residuals accumulate as a result either of the spread between the cash flows from the collateral and the cash flows to the tranches or of conservative prepayment and reinvestment assumptions. Residual cash flows are apportioned to the originating financial institution or to investors that hold subordinate rights.

In exchange for a fee, a guarantor assumes an obligation to pay cash if the mortgagors default. In some cases, each underlying mortgage loan is guaranteed. In other cases, the entire pool is guaranteed. Guarantees often are only for a portion of the amount due (e.g., the first 20 percent). A servicer of the mortgage pool collects payments, deducts a fee, and passes through the remainder to the trust. The financial institution that originates the transaction may act as guarantor, as servicer, or both. Termination of the trust results in cash flows to the financial institution and to investors that hold subordinate rights.

Financial Instruments

The 1987 Exposure Draft provides the following definitions of financial instrument, financial asset, and financial liability which are expected to be helpful in recognition and measurement issues as well as disclosure (FASB [1987b], paras. 27–29):

A financial instrument is any contract that is both a (recognized or unrecognized) financial asset of one entity and a (recognized or unrecognized) financial liability of another entity.

A financial asset is any asset that is (a) cash, (b) a contractual right to receive cash or another financial asset from another entity, (c) a contractual right to exchange other financial instruments on potentially favorable terms with another entity, or (d) an equity instrument of another entity.

A financial liability is any liability that is a contractual obligation to (a) deliver cash or another financial asset to another entity or (b) exchange financial instruments on potentially unfavorable terms with another entity.

FIGURE 2

Components of Financial Instruments

1. *Receivable (Payable)*—An unconditional right (obligation) to receive (deliver) cash or another financial asset.

2. *Conditional Receivable (Payable)*—A right (obligation) to receive (deliver) cash or another financial asset that is conditional upon the occurrence of an event.

3. *Forward Contract*—An unconditional right and obligation to exchange other financial instruments.

4. *Guarantee or Other Conditional Exchange*—A right and obligation to exchange other financial instruments that is conditional upon the occurrence of an event outside the control of either party to the contract.

5. *Option*—A right (obligation) to exchange other financial instruments that is conditional upon the occurrence of an event within the control of one party to the contract.

6. *Equity Instrument*—An ownership interest that becomes a right (obligation) to receive (deliver) cash or other financial (or nonfinancial) assets only on the condition of liquidation.

Those definitions reflect various contractual rights or obligations to receive, deliver, or exchange financial instruments. Those rights or obligations may be unconditional, or they may be conditioned on the occurrence of an event. However, rights and obligations are necessarily paired, as are conditions. The trust in Figure 1 that holds the rights to the pool of mortgage loans holds a financial asset because the mortgagor of each loan in that pool has a financial liability. The right of the trust to receive cash from the guarantor and the guarantor's obligation to deliver cash are conditioned on defaults by mortgagors.

Components

The FASB staff is developing an approach for analyzing recognition and measurement issues in accounting for financial instruments. That approach views all financial instruments as being made up of a few basic components or types of contracts and assumes that accounting issues related to financial instruments can be resolved by analyzing complex instruments into their basic components and by focusing on those components.

Financial instruments can be viewed as consisting of one or more fundamental components that convey rights and obligations. A list of six components is presented in Figure 2.

The components in Figure 2 can be used to identify and analyze the combination of rights and obligations conveyed by a financial instrument. For example, a typical mortgage loan contract conveys several rights and obligations. For a mortgagor (borrower), that contract may convey (1) obligations to pay specified amounts of cash at specified future dates (payables);

(2) rights to prepay, that is, to exchange a specified amount of cash for settlement of all or some of the payables if the mortgagor wants to make the exchange (call options held); (3) obligations to exchange the mortgaged property for the settlement of some or all of the obligations if the mortgagor defaults (guarantees); (4) obligations to pay an insurance company to maintain a specified amount of insurance coverage (payables); (5) obligations to settle the obligations if the property is destroyed by an insured event (conditional payables); and (6) obligations to exchange cash for the settlement of the obligations if the property is destroyed in an uninsured event (guarantees).

A financial institution (lender) may recognize "mortgage loans receivable" as an asset on its statement of financial position, but the typical contract underlying that receivable includes not only unconditional rights to receive cash at specified future dates but also and obligations to exchange that are conditional on the occurrence of specified events. For the financial institution, that same contract may convey (1) rights to receive a specified amount of cash on specified future dates (receivables); (2) obligations to accept prepayment, that is, to exchange the receivable for cash if the mortgagor wants to make the exchange (call options written); (3) rights to exchange some or all of the receivables for the mortgaged property if the mortgagor defaults (guarantees); and (4) rights to exchange the receivable for cash from either the mortgagor or the insurance company if the property is destroyed (guarantees). Instead of recognizing a single "mortgage loans receivable," the rights and obligations associated with the components could be recognized:

Guarantee—insurance
Guarantee—default
Receivable
    Call option—prepayments

The components in Figure 2 also can be used to identify the transactions and financial instruments used to securitize assets. The transaction used to convey to investors the rights to the cash flows from the pool of mortgage loans can be recognized either as a sale of the underlying collateral (pool of mortgage loans) or as a secured borrowing. Different components are associated with each alternative.

Several components are reflected if that transaction is recognized as a sale. The components associated with the "mortgage loans receivable," including the unconditional rights to receive cash at specified dates and the conditional rights and obligations to exchange described above, are conveyed to the trust. In exchange, the financial institution received cash, acquired or retained subordinated rights, and incurred an obligation to exchange cash or other financial assets if defective documentation exists. That transaction could be reflected in the following journal entry:

    Cash
    Subordinated rights
    Call option—prepayments
            Receivable
            Guarantee—default
            Guarantee—insurance
            Guarantee—documentation
            Gain (loss) on sale

The subordinated rights may represent rights to receive cash if funds remain in the collection account after each required semiannual payment of interest and principal to the investors (a conditional receivable), or they may represent rights to receive cash only on the occasion of the liquidation of the trust (an equity instrument if the trust is considered to be a separate entity). The obligation to exchange cash or financial assets if defective documentation exists may be conditional on an event that is outside the control of either party (guarantee).

Several different components also are reflected if that transaction is viewed as a secured borrowing. One component is an unconditional obligation to deliver cash at specified future dates (a payable). Another is the obligation to deliver cash or other financial assets that is conditional on the occurrence of an event—prepayments (a conditional payable). A third is the obligation to relinquish the collateral (the pool of mortgage loans) if the financial institution defaults (a guarantee). Other components may reflect a right to exchange cash for the settlement of some or all of the remaining payables at specified future dates if the mortgagors make prepayments (a guarantee) and a right to exchange cash for the remaining payables at specified future dates if the principal amount of the payables then outstanding is less than a specified minimum amount and the issuer wants to make the exchange (a held call option). Those components could be reflected in the following journal entry:

Cash

    Guarantee—prepayments
    Call option
            Payable—senior rights
            Conditional payable—subordinate rights
            Guarantee—collateral

The components associated with the "mortgage loans receivable," including the unconditional rights to receive cash at specified dates as well as the conditional rights and obligations to exchange described above, are conveyed to the trust but are viewed as being retained by the financial institution.

Recognition and Measurement

A threshold question is whether the exchange with investors should be recognized as a sale of the underlying collateral or as a secured borrowing. Accountants frequently debate the form versus substance of an exchange transaction. The substance of the exchange is whether the probable future benefits and related inherent risks embodied in the collateral have been transferred. However, the form of the exchange usually affects its accounting treatment.

FASB Technical Bulletin (TB) 85-2, *Accounting for Collateralized Mortgage Obligations (CMOs)* (FASB [1985b]), applies to certain types of bonds secured by mortgage loans such as collateralized mortgage obligations that are structured so that all or substantially all of the collections of principal and interest from the underlying collateral are passed through to holders of the bonds. Paragraph 2 of TB 85-2 concludes as follows about how those bonds should be accounted for:

> CMOs should be presumed to be borrowings that are reported as liabilities in the financial statements of the issuer unless all but a nominal portion of the future economic benefits inherent in the associated collateral have been irrevocably passed to the investor and no affiliate of the issuer can be required to make future payments with respect to the obligation. The existence of all of the following conditions at the date of issuance of the CMO would generally indicate that the borrowing presumption has been overcome, that the associated collateral should be eliminated from the issuer's financial statements, and that gain or loss should be recognized:
>
> a. The issuer and its affiliates surrender the future economic benefits embodied in the collateral securing the obligation.
>   (1) Neither the issuer nor its affiliates have the right or obligation to substitute collateral or obtain it by calling the obligation.
>   (2) The expected residual interest, if any, in the collateral is nominal.
> b. No affiliate of the issuer can be required to make any future payments with respect to the obligation.
>   (1) The investor can look only to the issuer's assets or third parties

(such as insurers or guarantors) for repayment of both principal and interest on the obligation, and neither the sponsor of the issuer nor its other affiliates are secondarily liable.

(2) Neither the issuer nor its affiliates can be required to redeem the obligation prior to its stated maturity other than through the normal pay-through of collections from the collateral.

If the associated collateral is eliminated from the financial statements because all of the above conditions are met, any expected residual interest in the collateral should not be recognized as an asset. Rather, such residual interest should be recorded as it accrues to the benefit of the issuer or its affiliates . . . [footnotes omitted].

Sales treatment for CMOs is allowed under TB 85-2 even though the transactions purport to be borrowings, but only if probable future benefits and all related inherent risks embodied in the collateral have been transferred. Subordinated rights to residual cash flows should be nominal and are not to be recognized as an asset.

FASB Statement No. 77, *Reporting by Transferors for Transfers of Receivables with Recourse* (FASB [1983b]), specifies that a transferor should report a transfer of receivables with recourse as a sale if it purports to be a sale and all of the following conditions are met:

a. The transferor surrenders control of the future economic benefits embodied in the receivables. Control has not been surrendered if the transferor has an option to repurchase the receivables at a later date.

b. The transferor's obligation under the recourse provisions can be reasonably estimated. Lack of experience with receivables with characteristics similar to those being transferred or other factors that affect a determination at the transfer date of the collectibility of the receivables may impair the ability to make a reasonable estimate of the probable bad debt losses and related costs of collections and repossessions. A transfer of receivables shall not be recognized as a sale if collectibility of the receivables and related costs of collection and repossession are not subject to reasonable estimation.

c. The transferee cannot require the transferor to repurchase the receivables except pursuant to the recourse provisions. [Para. 5, footnotes omitted]

If those conditions do not exist, the proceeds from the transfer should be reported as a liability.

Statement 77 applies to exchanges that purport to be sales or are structured as sales agreements. Because CMOs are not structured as sales agreements but as debt instruments collateralized by mortgage or mortgage-backed loans, Statement 77 does not apply to CMOs. However, some important inconsistencies between TB 85-2 and Statement 77 suggest several recognition and measurement issues that will have to be resolved as part of the financial instruments project.

A transferor that retains more than insignificant and trifling future economic benefits and retains any related risks cannot treat the transfer as a sale under TB 85-2. Yet a transferor can retain some future economic benefits and all of the related risks and treat the transfer as a sale under Statement 77. When is the underlying collateral (the pool of mortgage loans) considered sold? Were the future economic benefits and related risks associated with collateral transferred?

Both TB 85-2 and Statement 77 emphasize legal form rather than whether the probable future economic benefits and related risks have been retained by the transferor. If those benefits and risks accrue only to the transferor, its financial well-being will be affected by the amount and timing of principal and interest payments by mortgagors. Investors will be indifferent about where their cash receipts come from. Alternatively, if those benefits and risks do not accrue to the transferor, its financial well-being will not be affected by those payments by mortgagors.

It is unlikely that all of the probable future economic benefits and related risks associated with the collateral will accrue or will not accrue only to the transferor. Instead, those benefits and risks will be shared among the parties to the exchange in some agreed-on fashion. The question then becomes, What benefits and risks have been transferred? Identification of the basic components or types of contracts facilitates an analysis and assessment of how those benefits and risks will be shared.

Should sales treatment be precluded if some risks such as credit risk and guarantees of quality are retained by the transferor? Is retention of any risk by itself sufficient to preclude sales treatment? In the situation presented in Figure 1, the financial institution has incurred an obligation to exchange cash or other financial assets if defective documentation exists. However, no obligation has been incurred by that institution for failure of the mortgagors to make principal and interest payments when due or for the effects of prepayments.

TB 85-2 precludes sales treatment for an exchange if the transferor retains credit risk. In contrast, FASB Statement No. 5, *Accounting for Contingencies* (FASB [1975]), allows sales recognition if the collectibility of the receivables and related costs of collection and repossession are subject to reasonable estimation. Also, FASB Statement No. 48, *Revenue Recognition When Right of Return Exists* (FASB [1981b]), does not preclude sales treatment for an exchange in which a right of future return exists if the seller can reasonably estimate the amount of those returns. Similarly, Statement 77 does not preclude sales treatment for an exchange in which credit risk is retained if the transferor can reasonably estimate its obligations under the recourse provisions.

Should sales treatment be precluded if some probable future economic benefits are retained by the transferor? Is retention of those benefits by itself sufficient to preclude sales treatment? In the situation presented in Figure 1, the financial institution has transferred control over the collateral to the trustee, has received cash, and has received or retained subordinated rights to receive cash that are conditional on the occurrence of specified events. Those rights are to the residual cash flows that result from any initial overcollateralization, the excess cash flows from greater prepayments than expected, and reinvestment earnings on both of the preceding items between bond payment dates. Those residual cash flows often can be reasonably estimated at the inception of the transaction, but the actual outcomes may differ from initial estimates because of future conditions such as the actual rate of prepayments and actual reinvestment rates.

There are precedents in the accounting literature for treating an exchange transaction as a sale even though the seller retains rights to residual cash flows. For example, under FASB Statement No. 13, *Accounting for Leases* (FASB [1976]), an unguaranteed residual value accruing to the benefit of the lessor does not preclude accounting for the lease as a sales-type or direct financing lease. If at least 90 percent of the fair value of the leased asset will be recovered through future minimum lease payments, Statement 13 requires a lessor to account for a leasing transaction as a sales-type or direct financing lease as long as collectibility of the minimum lease payments is reasonably predictable and there are no important uncertainties about the amount of unreimbursable costs yet to be incurred by the lessor. In those cases, the present value of the unguaranteed residual value is included in the balance sheet carrying amount of the net investment in that lease. The final amount of the residual value in the leased property that reverts to the lessor at the end of the lease term does not affect the initial accounting for the transaction. As a result, Statement 13 effectively allows the lessor to retain title to the underlying asset, to retain up to 10 percent of the benefits and risks inherent in the asset, and to retain an unlimited final residual interest in the leased property, and still account for the transaction as a sale or financing.

Under FASB Statement No. 66, *Accounting for Sales of Real Estate* (FASB [1982b]), the retention of a residual interest in real property, such as participation in operating profits or residual values without further obligation, does not impede the recognition of profit under the full accrual method. Paragraph 43 of that Statement states that "if the transaction otherwise qualifies for recognition of profit by the full accrual method, the transfer of risks and rewards of ownership and absence of continuing involvement criteria shall be considered met."

Under FASB Statement No. 76, *Extinguishment of Debt* (FASB [1983a]), the essentially risk-free assets transferred to an independent trustee by a debtor must be used solely for satisfying scheduled principal and interest payments and must produce cash flows that approximately coincide with the debt service requirements. As a result, the amount of residual interest that the debtor is allowed to retain in the transferred collateral is limited only by the requirement that the associated cash flows approximately coincide. Because the residual interest cannot be withdrawn from the trust by the debtor until the obligation has been fully satisfied, it can accumulate into a substantial amount.

Statement 77 requires that the transferor surrender "control of the future economic benefits embodied in the receivables." However, that Statement also applies to "transfers of specified interests in a pool of receivables," and some believe that an issuer can retain the risks and some of the rewards of future interest rate changes, a significant portion of the interest payments, and auxiliary benefits such as specified prepayment penalties and still treat the exchange as a sale.

If the transferor's retention of some probable future economic benefits and some related risks does not preclude sales treatment, should the rights to those benefits and the obligations for those risks be recognized? TB 85-2 precludes the recognition as an asset of the expected residual interest in the collateral. That residual interest is recorded as it accrues. Similarly, participation in operating profits or residual values without further obligations are recognized as realized under Statement 66, and any residual interest that a debtor is allowed to retain under Statement 76 is recorded as it accrues. However, if a lease is treated as a sales-type or direct financing lease by a lessor, under Statement 13 the present value of the unguaranteed residual value is included in the balance sheet carrying amount of the investment in that lease. Obligations for credit risk under Statement 77 and for a right of return under Statement 48 are recognized when amounts for those obligations can be reasonably measured.

If the transferor's retention of some probable future economic benefits and some related risks precludes sales treatment, can the obligations recognized qualify for debt extinguishment treatment? Statement 76 specifies that debt is considered extinguished if the debtor is relieved of primary liability for the debt by the creditor and it is probable that the debt will not be required to make future payments as guarantor of the debt. Statement 76 also specifies that, even though the creditor does not relieve the debtor of its primary obligation, debt is to be considered extinguished if the debtor irrevocably places cash or other essentially risk-free monetary assets in a trust solely for satisfying that debt and the possibility that the debtor will be required to make further payments is remote.

The collateral used to secure the mortgage debt obligations may have essentially no credit risk because of government guarantees but would not qualify as "essentially risk-free" because of prepayment risk. However, that risk can be effectively eliminated by passing prepayments through to investors. Moreover, since the collateral has been transferred to a trust without recourse and investors have agreed to look only to the collateral held by the trust for satisfaction of the obligations, it can be argued that the transferor is not primarily liable for those obligations and should account for the obligations as extinguished regardless of the nature and quality of the assets held in the trust. However, FASB Technical Bulletin No. 84-4, *In-Substance Defeasance of Debt* (FASB [1984]), prohibits off–balance sheet treatment for instantaneous in-substance defeasances of debt because they are "borrow-and-invest" transactions. That pronouncement states that "debt may not be extinguished through an in-substance defeasance if the assets that the debtor irrevocably places in trust were acquired at about the time that the debt was incurred or were acquired as part of a series of investment activities . . . initiated about the time that the debt was incurred." The exchange transaction used to securitize assets could be characterized as an invest-and-borrow transaction even if the criteria and conditions in Statement 76 are satisfied.

Discussion and Conclusions

The approach being considered by the FASB will attempt to analyze recognition and measurement issues for financial instruments by focusing on the components of those instruments that convey rights and obligations. That approach will (1) identify fundamental components, (2) determine whether to recognize and how to measure those components, (3) analyze complex financial instruments as aggregations of those components, and (4) determine whether to recognize and how to measure complex financial instruments by considering the accounting for those components as well as the effects of relationships between financial instruments. The intent of that approach is to focus on the economic substance of the rights and obligations conveyed by financial instruments which may or may not be described by the legal form of those instruments and to properly reflect the effects of those rights and obligations in the financial statements.

The need for that type of approach is reflected in the issue summary for Emerging Issues Task Force (EITF) Issue 86-24 (FASB [1987a]). A financial institution sold mortgage loans to an unrelated third party that used the loans as collateral for CMOs issued through a special-purpose entity. The mortgage loans were sold without recourse, but the financial institution acquired rights to residual cash flows as part of the transaction. The EITF concluded that the mortgage loans should be accounted for as a sale by the financial institution. The FASB staff viewed the transaction as a financing. The SEC observer indicated that the SEC staff may challenge these transactions on a fact-specific basis if they are not reported in a manner consistent with their economic substance.

But how should we determine the economic substance of a financial instrument? There is an old saying that ''the approach to a problem is often more important than its solution.'' The proposed approach will try to focus on the components inherent in a financial instrument—the rights and obligations conveyed—as a way to diagnose the economic substance of that instrument. That approach is similar to the approach used in pricing and evaluating financial instruments. For example, Kao (1988) suggests that an evaluation of newly created financial instruments includes two stages: (1) break down the instrument into its individual components (while maintaining similar overall risk/return profile) and (2) evaluate the relative price of each component with techniques such as ''what if'' analysis, interest sensitivity analysis, and option pricing analysis.

There is another old saying that ''when working toward the solution of a problem, it always helps if you know the answer.'' At this point, we don't know the answer, and we can't be sure that the proposed approach will help us to know the answer. Several difficulties can be anticipated.

One difficulty is likely to be the identification of components. An analysis of the transactions and financial instruments summarized in Figure 1 suggests that different components can be identified if the exchange transaction used to securitize assets is recognized as a sale or as a secured borrowing. Only the amount of cash received by the financial institution is common to the two accounting treatments. Should the accounting treatment for the exchange transaction be used to determine the identity of the fundamental components, should the identity of those components be used to determine the accounting treatment for the exchange transaction, or are the identification of components and the accounting treatment for the exchange transaction related interdependently?

Another difficulty is likely to be the generality of the accounting recognition, measurement, and derecognition of fundamental components. Should the accounting for a given component be the same in all situations, or should there be exceptions? For example, options written could be initially recognized as liabilities and measured at the explicit premium received. Yet some believe that an option that is deep-in-the-money at issuance may be something more than just an option and perhaps should be considered to be an exception.

Similarly, unconditional receivables or payables could be initially recognized as assets or liabilities and measured at their present value or surrogate for that amount. Accounting Principles Board Opinion No. 21, *Interest on Receivables and Payables* (APB [1971]), requires that notes received or issued for cash be reported at their present value as measured by their cash proceeds and that notes exchanged for property, goods, or services be reported at the present value of the consideration exchanged. However, that Opinion makes important exceptions for trade receivables and payables not exceeding approximately one year, advance payments for goods and services, security deposits, customary lending and deposit activities of financial institutions, transactions that reflect interest rates that are affected by governmental restrictions or taxes, and transactions between a parent company and its subsidiaries. Should those exceptions continue in measuring unconditional receivables and payables?

Other difficulties are likely to arise as the fundamental components are combined into complex financial instruments and the relationships between financial instruments are considered. The proposed approach is similar to the approach used by the FASB to analyze transfers of receivables with recourse.

Paragraph 21 of Statement 77 focuses on the rights and obligations resulting from those transfers. However, some believe that in developing recognition and measurement criteria for those transfers, the FASB placed too much reliance on a notion of control and too much emphasis on the legal form of the transfer (Stewart and Neuhausen [1986]).

There is yet another old saying that "the approach to a problem often changes the nature of the problem." In analyzing complex financial instruments, there is a tendency to focus on the guarantees, options, equity rights, and conditional receivables or payables. We assume that we know how to account for unconditional receivables or payables. Yet if the risks and rewards of a receivable—the most basic fundamental component—can be separated, fragmented, recombined, and partially transferred, how do we account for what is transferred and what is retained? Perhaps this is what people have had in mind when they have criticized current standards as being driven more by legal form than by economic substance. They may have been concerned about our understanding of and accounting for the basic unconditional receivable component of a financial instrument. The proposed approach will expose all of the components for analysis, and resolution of issues about how to account for those components may help us develop consistent guidance for the financial instruments that include those components.

The exchange transaction used to create securitized assets does not reflect a discrete event or a discrete contract. It would be much easier to account for that exchange transaction if the underlying contract was of short duration, required limited involvement and interactions among the parties, focused on easily measured objects of exchange, anticipated a minimum of future cooperation, and required no future sharing of benefits and risks. However, that transaction initiates a set of ongoing contractual relations that will be of long duration, will require relations and interactions among the parties, will focus on some objects of exchange that cannot be easily measured, will anticipate some ongoing interaction of behavior and cooperation among the parties, will anticipate some troubles and difficulties, and will require future sharing of benefits and risks. The nature of those ongoing contractual relations greatly complicates any analysis of the economic substance of the rights and obligations conveyed. That is the challenge we face in accounting for securitized assets—to understand and account for that substance in the context of the contractual relations among the parties.

Disclosure

The November 1987 Exposure Draft (FASB [1987]) broadly defined financial instruments to include both instruments for which the potential risk of loss is the amount recognized in the statement of financial position (for example, bonds, loans, and trade receivables and payables) and instruments with potential risk of accounting loss that may substantially exceed the amount recognized, if any, in the statement of financial position (for example, interest rate swaps, forward contracts to buy or sell government bonds, and loan commitments).

The 1987 Exposure Draft proposed to require for all financial instruments disclosure of information about their credit risk (maximum credit risk, probable and reasonably possible credit losses, and individual, industry, or geographic concentrations); market risk, including interest rate and foreign exchange risks (effective interest rates and contractual repricing or maturity dates); liquidity risk (contractual future cash receipts and payments); and current market values if they could be determined or estimated.

After issuing the 1987 Exposure Draft, the FASB staff worked with a group of companies and accounting firms that participated in a test application of the Exposure Draft's provisions, met with financial analysts, accounting and other professional groups, and representatives of agencies that regulate financial institutions, and analyzed approximately 450 letters of comment received on the Exposure Draft to obtain a better understanding of the feasibility of implementing the proposed disclosure requirements, the potential implementation costs, and the usefulness of the resulting information.

Overall, most respondents agreed that improving disclosure of information about financial instruments was a useful interim step pending completion of the recognition and measurement phases of the financial instruments project. Most respondents agreed in general with the purposes of disclosure set forth in the 1987 Exposure Draft and that the areas of risk identified need more comparable disclosure of information.

However, many respondents asserted that the proposed disclosure requirements were too extensive and too costly to implement. They also asserted that off-balance sheet issues were not sufficiently considered in the Exposure Draft. They noted that many of the proposed requirments (for example, future contractual receipts and payments and information about interest rates and foreign exchange rates) generally could not be applied to some financial instruments with off-balance sheet risk because of the contingent or conditional nature of those instruments.

After considering those responses, the FASB concluded that the most expeditious way to resolve what many respondents perceived as the area most in need of improvement was to consider the disclosure issues discussed in the 1987 Exposure Draft in two phases. The first phase principally considers financial instruments with off-balance sheet risk, focusing on disclosing information about the extent, nature and terms of the entity's use of those instruments, as well as related information about credit risk. That phase also addresses concentrations of credit risk for all financial instruments. The second phase focuses on all financial instruments and disclosure of information about the credit, market, and liquidity risk of those instruments.

In July 1989, the FASB issued an Exposure Draft of a proposed Statement, Disclosure of Information about Financial Instruments with Off-Balance-Sheet Risk and Financial Instruments with Concentrations of Credit Risk (FASB [1989]). That proposed Statement would require disclosure of information about the following for financial instruments with off-balance sheet risk:

The face, contract, or notional principal amount and the amount recognized in the statement of financial position.

The nature and terms of the instruments and a discussion of the credit, market, and liquidity risk and related accounting policies.

The loss the entity would incur if any counterparty to the financial instrument failed to perform.

The entity's policy for requiring collateral or other security on financial instruments it accepts and a description of collateral on instruments presently held.

The proposed Statement also would require disclosure of information about concentrations of credit risk for all financial instruments. The disclosures would be effective for calendar-year 1989 for all requirements except disclosure of collateral and concentration information, which would be required for 1990.

Recognition and Measurement

The FASB is using a "building block" approach in considering recognition and measurement issues for financial instruments and has been discussing unconditional receivables (payables) and options—two of the building block instruments. The FASB has tentatively concluded that unconditional receivables (payables) should be measured initially at an estimated market value, such as the present value of the expected future cash flow discounted at a market rate of interest; the stated transaction value would continue to be an appropriate initial measure for the many receivables and payables for which stated transaction value approximates estimated market value. The FASB also has tentatively concluded that current market value provides more relevant information on subsequently measuring unconditional receivables and payables, assuming that a sufficiently reliable market value can be determined at reasonable cost.

The FASB's discussion of options has focused on financial options that are not considered to be hedges of other financial instruments, are not embedded in compound financial instruments, or are not held or written by an entity on its own stock. The FASB has tentatively concluded that options written and held should be recognized as liabilities and assets, respectively. It also has tentatively concluded that options that are traded in auction or dealer markets should be subsequently measured at current market value, and other options should be subsequently measured at estimated current market value—estimated by use of such methods as option pricing models and matrix pricing techniques—if feasible. Finally, the FASB has tentatively concluded that when options expire, are sold or transferred, are cancelled by mutual agreement, or are exercised, the carrying amount of the option should be removed from the statement of financial position; the newly acquired asset, if any, should be initially measured by its market value at exercise; and any remaining carrying amount of the option should generally be recognized as a gain or loss.

An eventual step will be to test the FASB's tentative conclusions for building block instruments by using them as the basis for considering recognition and measurement issues for compound instruments. For example, the FASB's tentative conclusions about options and unconditional receivables (payables) could be tested by focusing on a callable zero coupon bond or a certificate of deposit that can be redeemed early at the holder's option.

REFERENCES

Accounting Principles Board. Opinion No. 21, *Interest on Receivables and Payables.* AICPA, 1971.
Brown, Peter G., Thomas A. Zimmerman, and K. Jeanne Person. "Introduction to Mortgages and Mortgage-Backed Securities." Salomon Brothers, 1987.
Bryan, Lowell L. "The Selling of America's Loans." *The Wall Street Journal.* October 20, 1986.
———. The Credit Bomb in Our Credit System." *Harvard Business Review,* January–February 1987, pp. 45–51.
———. *Breaking Up the Bank: Rethinking an Industry under Siege.* Dow-Jones, 1988.
Ellwood, Don C. "REMICS, Residuals and Stripped Mortgage Securities." *Financial Instruments Memorandum No. 1.* Arthur Young, 1987.
Financial Accounting Standards Board. Statement No. 5, *Accounting for Contingencies.* FASB, 1975.
———. Statement No. 13, *Accounting for Leases.* FASB, 1976.
———. Exposure Draft, *Accounting and Reporting by Transferors for Transfers of Receivables with Recourse.* FASB, 1981a.
———. Statement No. 48, *Revenue Recognition When Right of Return Exists.* FASB, 1981b.
———. Revised Exposure Draft, *Reporting by Transferors for Transfers of Receivables with Recourse.* FASB, 1982a.
———. Statement No. 66, *Accounting for Sales of Real Estate.* FASB, 1982b.
———. Statement No. 76, *Extinguishment of Debt.* FASB, 1983a.
———. Statement No. 77, *Reporting by Transferors for Transfers of Receivables with Recourse.* FASB, 1983b.
———. Technical Bulletin No. 84-4, *In-Substance Defeasance of Debt.* FASB, 1984.
———. Concepts Statement No. 6, *Elements of Financial Statements.* FASB, 1985a.
———. Technical Bulletin No. 85-2, *Accounting for Collateralized Mortgage Obligations (CMOs).* FASB, 1985b.
———. *EITF Abstracts.* FASB, 1987a.
———. Exposure Draft, *Disclosures about Financial Instruments.* FASB. 1987.
———. Exposure Draft, *Disclosures about Financial Instruments.* FASB, 1987b.
———. Exposure Draft, *Disclosure of Information about Financial Instruments with Off-Balance Sheet Risk and Financial Instruments with Concentrations of Credit Risk.* FASB. 1989.
Ijiri, Yuji. FASB Research Report, *Recognition of Contractual Rights and Obligations: An Exploratory Study of Conceptual Issues.* FASB, 1980.
Kao, Duen-Li. "Investment Innovations and Dangers." *Journal of Cash Management,* March–April 1988, pp. 42–44.
Stewart, John E., and Benjamin S. Neuhausen. "Financial Instruments and Transactions: The CPA's Newest Challenge." *Journal of Accountancy,* August 1986, pp. 102–112.

Discussion of Recognition and Measurement Issues in Accounting for Securitized Assets

GERALD I. WHITE*

As Ben Neuhausen has provided an excellent technical commentary on the issues involved in the project on financial instruments, I would like to make my comments more general in nature. I would like to start by making clear my bias. As one who uses financial statements to make investment decisions, my perspective is that of one primarily concerned with the information content of financial statements.

With respect to financial instruments, it is apparent to me that current standards are totally inadequate. Current disclosure is spotty at best, and, in many cases, comparability is lacking. For example, twelve oil companies and other major buyers of steel pipe used for oil drilling signed major "take-or-pay" contracts with U.S. Steel in the late 1970s in order to induce U.S. Steel to build a new mill. These agreements were used to induce lenders to supply the financing for the mill. When the mill was opened a few years later, drill pipe was in oversupply. Despite extensive reading of annual reports, I have found only one company that discloses this obligation.

The proliferation of financial instruments is a function of dynamic markets. Such innovation is, in part, economic: the need for new instruments to meet economic needs. However, the growth of financial instruments is also, clearly, responsive to regulatory concerns. For banks, products that do not impact capital ratios are especially desirable in a capital-short world.

Accounting considerations also play a major role in the creation of new instruments. Leasing activity is impacted by FASB Statement 13; lease terms are tailored to place the lease on the desired side of the line between leases that must be capitalized and those that are not.

It is for this reason that many users believe that disclosure is more important than accounting standards. With adequate disclosure, analysts can make their own decisions and their own adjustments to reported data. From this perspective, the SEC requirement to disclose leases (Accounting Series Release No. 147) was more significant than FASB Statement 13.

Users are also concerned that accounting sometimes favors form over

---

*President, Grace & White, Inc.

substance. Ben Neuhausen already mentioned one example—the sale of receivables with recourse. It is clear to me that when partial recourse is effectively full recourse, then the "sale" is in reality collateralized borrowing.

Where disclosure is adequate, users can create their own balance sheets, debt ratios, and so forth. Whether disclosure is sufficient is a problem for standards setters and regulators. The answer hinges, I believe, on whether or not one believes that the income statement and balance sheet are supposed to be meaningful representations of income and net worth.

As many of you are academics, I think that it is worthwhile to point out that the financial instruments project will provide data that may be useful to you as well. I believe there is a great need for research based on actual financial statements. The data provided by companies on their financial risks should permit, for example, testing of the relationship between risk and market valuation.

As Panel Discussant (Session III)

As I had an opportunity this morning to make some general comments, I would like to make specific comments regarding some of the papers given today.

I found the Gorton and Pennacchi paper somewhat disturbing. (I mean that as a compliment.) If, in fact, there is an implicit guarantee given to the loan buyer, then the accounting for such sales is, at best, deceptive.

One quibble with the paper, however. I see no reason to treat the loans of nonpublic borrowers differently. As long as financial statements are available, the loans of such borrowers can be evaluated just as well as those of public entities.

Regarding the Glick and Plaut work, I have somewhat greater concerns. In my experience, many companies seek both excess liquidity and bank credit lines at the same time; both are the result of a conservative "corporate personality." Such companies are willing to bear the cost of surplus liquidity.

When interest rates rise, they will pursue credit lines in order to tie up liquidity "in case it is needed." At the same time they may shift liquid assets into higher yielding near-monies. Thus, the data Glick and Plaut produce may be explained by an alternative hypothesis.

Of course, the market has come to understand that measures of the money supply leave much to be desired; financial markets no longer pay any attention to these data.

I found the research by El-Gazzar et al. quite interesting. It would be even more interesting to see the study updated. I would like to think that the issuance of Statement 13 resulted in greater awareness of the lease issue among lenders and that subsequently negotiated covenants took leases into account more often.

Discussion of Recognition and Measurement Issues in Accounting for Securitized Assets

NICHOLAS DOPUCH* AND GRACE POWNALL*

As academics, the first task facing us was to determine the general approach to follow in developing our discussion comments on Bob Swieringa's paper. This is not as straightforward as one might assume since Swieringa's paper does not fit the typical mold of a research or academic paper which we would normally be asked to discuss. Instead, the paper reflects the interests and concerns of one who grapples on a full-time basis with the practical and theoretical problems encountered in establishing financial accounting standards.

Upon reflection, we came to the conclusion that we lack both the requisite expertise and the interest to debate many of the technical points covered in Swieringa's paper. We believe that we can provide a more useful discussion by focusing on the broader issues of whether a new FASB standard is needed in the area of securitized assets, and what effects a new standard in this area might have on the preparation and dissemination of information by firms engaged in such transactions and the interpretation of that information by investors and other members of the financial community.

At the outset, we wish to emphasize that our choice of this strategy should not be viewed in any way as a reflection of a basic dissatisfaction with Bob's paper. As a matter of fact, we believe the paper does an excellent job of providing a comprehensive presentation of the issues being debated by members of the FASB concerning this potential accounting problem, and discussing the pros and cons of adopting different positions on these issues. As such, the paper is clearly an improvement over the FASB's Exposure Draft (ED) on this issue issued in November 1987. Indeed, the confusion we encountered in reading that ED was the first motivating force leading us to adopt a more general approach to developing our discussion comments.

More specifically, we believe that the confusion we encountered with the ED is simply a manifestation of how the FASB's incremental approach to setting disclosure and measurement standards has brought us to a morass regarding the current state of accounting regulations. There seems to be no

*Washington University, St. Louis, Mo.

limit to the kinds of measurements and disclosures that might qualify for inclusion in financial accounting standards (FASs). For example, on page 67 Swieringa states that the issues to be addressed in the financial instruments project will include consideration of how to account for transactions "that seek to transfer market or credit risks, including hedges, options, commitments, nonrecourse arrangements, and guarantees." Also he states that the measurement issues to consider include whether financial instruments "should be measured. . . . at market value, original cost, or lower of cost or market." The first quote indicates that the FASB feels capable of moving into any area of financial transactions, whether these entail valuations of future events that may or may not take place. The second quotation provides us with an indication of how far regulatory agencies have come since the 1960s regarding their willingness to adopt mixtures of historical costs, market values, replacement costs, or any other measurement system that might have current appeal.

This may seem to be an extreme, and perhaps unfair, characterization of the FASB's current state, but it is certainly consistent with the most recent FAS on income taxes (Statement No. 96, Accounting for Income Taxes). That standard forces firms' accountants and their auditors to compute what is labeled a liability for future income taxes that basically rests on a series of "as if" transactions that might occur in the future, based on predictions of firms' future optimal tax strategies, tax rates, "reversals," and so forth. The result is a very complex and elaborate measurement system employed to obtain an estimate of what many accountants have long argued is a fictitious liability to begin with. The interesting thing is that this and all other FASs, whether they deal with historical or future transactions or with past acquisition costs or future market values, can be justified by merely citing as a litany the conceptual framework of accounting (e.g., see Appendix B of the Financial Instruments ED). It is hard to believe that all unconstrained FASs can consistently fit within the same conceptual framework.

Indeed, that may well be the origin of our disagreement with the way in which the FASB intends to approach this controversy. That is, both Bob and the ED point out that some financial instruments may fit existing standards and that some of these existing standards may provide conflicting treatments of similar kinds of financial instruments. (The latter are spelled out in some detail by Stewart and Neuhausen [1986].) This suggests that the first order of business should be a systematic analysis of the extent to which the characteristics of different financial instruments are such that their accounting requirements fall within the bounds of existing standards or they are so peculiar they need to be addressed in a new standard. Some might argue that the "components approach" illustrated in Swieringa's paper is a step in that direction. However, that approach aims at a much more detailed kind of accounting than we typically are used to. In effect, the components approach tries to break down the accounting procedures for a financial asset/liability according to various rights/obligations depending on the different contingencies that might occur in the future. We wonder what it is about financial instruments that makes such an approach particularly useful since a components approach could conceivably be applied to other assets/liabilities in a similar way. For example, in estimating the market values of real estate assets held by pension funds, should the accountant estimate the total value as the sum of the market values of individual assets, as the sum of the values of blocks of related assets, or as a single market value (e.g., an entire shopping mall)? At a more mundane level, should accountants set up separate depreciation schedules for the individual parts of a machine, or should they depreciate the machine as a single asset? Some years ago, there was a proposal that fixed assets be recorded as two disaggregated values— one reflecting their value as operating assets and one reflecting their value as "tax shields." The latter would be "depreciated" at a rate consistent with the tax accounting treatment of the assets. Had accountants adopted this proposal, we wonder if the world would have been spared the controversial Statement 96.

Be that as it may, we suggest that a more useful approach at this point is to take each type of financial instrument discussed in the ED and ask whether that instrument could be recorded following existing rules and standards for asset/liability accounting, with specialized rights/obligations pertaining to these instruments reported as contingencies. Our opinion is that many of the contingencies would fit nicely under the umbrella of Statement No. 5, Accounting for Contingencies, which is a very broad standard. Surely, there are rules and standards that could cover many of the contingent rights associated with such instruments (e.g., similar to the rights associated with receivables "purchased" from other firms). In the process of reviewing which existing rules/standards can accommodate new or innovative financial instruments, the FASB would have an opportunity to discover and remove conflicting or redundant statements in existing standards before going on to issue new ones.

Bob's discussion of the accounting and reporting issues related to financial instruments suggests that the FASB is not averse to doing a full-scale review of existing standards before working on new ones. However, we read between the lines that somehow a decision has already been reached that even after doing so, a new standard will be needed to resolve these issues regardless of which old ones should be withdrawn or revised. We are skeptical that this need is there, particularly since our reading of Bob's paper did not allow us to gauge the extent to which so-called innovative financial instruments constitute a significant new problem in accounting. For example, although our guess is that financial institutions would be most affected by a new standard in this area, we could not ascertain whether and to what extent other entities would also be affected by such a standard. Similarly, the estimated dollar value of these kinds of transactions that escape current measurement and recognition standards is not provided, so we have little basis to assess the materiality of such "off-balance sheet" items. Finally, there are no explicit statements of what specific benefits can be expected to arise from a new standard dealing with contingent rights and obligations, nor of the costs of implementing that standard. We are confident such issues have been addressed by the Board, but the absence of specific references to them in Bob's paper or in the ED serves as a clue to the Board's predisposition in this area. As a consequence, our prediction is that the outcome of the FASB's deliberations on this project will essentially be another complex layer of regulations added to our current stock.

Given this general response to the ED and to Bob's paper, our recommendation is simply that the Board step back and first undertake an in-depth evaluation of the entire stock of financial accounting standards before issuing another Statement, particularly when this new Statement promises to extend accountants' involvement in additional "as if" transactions. A practical objective of this review might be to develop what could be called a 1989 version of ARB No. 43. This endeavor not only would improve everyone's thinking about what needs to be done regarding financial instruments, but should also highlight certain characteristics of our current stock of financial accounting standards, such as inconsistencies between them, the extent of overlaps, and trends in their scope and complexity. At the very least, the Board should broaden its perspective and consider an omnibus pronouncement covering disclosure, measurement, and recognition issues for all financial assets and financial liabilities. In addition to the standards and interpretations referred to in Bob's paper, the omnibus standard could also include sinking-fund assets (and their corresponding liabilities), pension assets and liabilities, and even long-term investments in the securities of nonconsolidated subsidiaries. With the general trend toward an increasing use of market values in accounting, why are long-term investments in unconsolidated subsidiaries carried at cost plus the parent's share of subsidiaries' undistributed incomes instead of at the current values of the investments? We do not wish this to be interpreted as a call for the additional use of market values in accounting. However, the trend in recent FASB standards certainly suggests that the Board does not recognize many constraints in employing market values (real and predicted) in different accounting areas. To some, including us, the move away from objective measurements in the more recent FASB standards is alarming, to say the least.

Not too long ago, the *Wall Street Journal* (August 3, 1988) carried a story indicating that the SEC is "quietly" investigating whether the FASB needs an "overhaul." Cited were accusations by critics that some of the more recent standards and some being proposed reflect a significant deficiency of benefits relative to their costs of implementation. A casual comparison of the length and complexity of the stock of financial accounting standards over time indicates that the standards are following the same evolutionary path as that associated with the Internal Revenue Code. If this continues, interested parties may again be motivated to consider some of the pros and cons of having a private accounting regulatory body continue to maintain control over the setting of accounting standards. The net benefits accruing from having the standards-setting process controlled by private regulatory agencies as opposed to public ones are starting to become blurred.

Discussion of Recognition and Measurement Issues in Accounting for Securitized Assets

Benjamin S. Neuhausen*

Dr. Swieringa's paper is a very good analysis of the existing accounting literature pertaining to accounting for securitized assets and of the conflicts and inconsistencies in that literature. In addition, his paper properly identifies the fundamental threshold question in accounting for securitized assets—"whether the exchange with investors should be recognized as a sale of the underlying collateral or as a secured borrowing." Raising the right question is a necessary first step to finding the right solution. Finally, the paper identifies the proper approach toward answering the threshold question by focusing on the economic substance of the exchange—"whether the probable future benefits and related inherent risks embodied in the collateral have been transferred." Thus, the paper sets forth a fundamentally sound approach to addressing the accounting issues in securitized asset transactions. My comments on the paper constitute suggested refinements to that basically sound approach.

First, although the paper contains a good summary of the existing accounting literature, it lacks any evaluation of the literature. We have had at least several years' experience with all of the authoritative documents cited in the paper. Which ones give more or less appropriate accounting results? We are not starting with a blank slate here; the accounting community has several years of experience with the existing literature. The FASB should try to benefit from that experience.

Second, the FASB should recognize that monetary assets are different from nonmonetary assets and that, as a result, the accounting standards relating to transactions involving nonmonetary assets may not be appropriate for similar transactions involving monetary assets. In other words, the differences in the nature of the two types of assets may support different accounting treatment for what on the surface appear to be similar transactions. The difference between monetary and nonmonetary assets lies in the much narrower range of rights and risks of ownership associated with monetary assets compared with nonmonetary assets. For a *monetary asset*, the

---

*Arthur Andersen & Co.

right of ownership is the right to collect interest and principal when due. The holder of that right stands to benefit if interest rates decline, because the value of those future cash flows increases; but that potential increase in value is always limited. Even if interest rates fall to zero, the value of the monetary asset can never exceed the undiscounted total of all future cash payments. The risks associated with owning a monetary asset are principally credit risk (the risk that interest, principal, or both will not be collected in a timely matter or at all) and interest rate risk (the risk that the value of the asset will decline because of rising interest rates or that the expected return will not be achieved because falling interest rates cause the debtor to prepay). By contrast, the owner of a *nonmonetary* asset has a broad array of rights and risks. He has rights to use that asset to generate income or other benefits, he may have the ability to use that nonmonetary asset in different ways or in different lines of business, and he stands to benefit from increases in value that are theoretically unlimited. The holder of a nonmonetary asset also is exposed to a number of risks of ownership—obsolescence, the possibility that the asset will become unsuitable for its intended use, destruction through casualty loss, defects in manufacturing or design, a change in the owner's business that renders the asset less useful or useless, and risks of decreased market value of the asset.

If a *nonmonetary* asset is sold and the seller provides the buyer with a warranty, that warranty exposes the seller to and protects the buyer against only one of several risks of ownership. In addition, in a sale of a nonmonetary asset with warranty, the rights of ownership clearly pass to the buyer. In a sale of a receivable for which the seller provides recourse to the buyer for credit losses (a warranty), the seller is retaining and the buyer is protected against a principal risk of ownership rather than just one of several. Further, in this situation it is not so clear who has the right of ownership to receive the future cash flows. Although the buyer will ultimately receive the cash from the debtor on the receivable, the receipt of cash is the same whether the buyer owns the receivable or lends money to the seller collateralized by the receivable. In summary, the narrower range of risks and rewards of ownership associated with monetary assets should be considered in determining the substance of securitization transactions and should be considered before analogizing to existing accounting standards for sales of nonmonetary assets.

Third, it is not clear to me that the components approach outlined in the paper is going to be useful in distinguishing sales from borrowings. The components approach appears to have promise in some of the other phases of the financial instruments project, but it may not be useful here, for four reasons:

- The definitions of the different components seem a little fuzzy, particularly the distinction between a conditional payable and a guarantee. A guarantee is defined as relating to the occurrence of an event outside the control of either party to the contract; by implication, a conditional payable relates to the occurrence of an event that is under the control of one party. When applying the definitions to the components of a mortgage, however, the mortgagor's obligation to surrender the property to the lender if the mortgagor defaults is described as a guarantee, even though the mortgagor controls his default. The obligation to pay off the loan if the property is destroyed in an insured event is described as a conditional payable, even though the insured event is outside the control of both the lender and the mortgagor.
- The components approach creates needless complexity with respect to the threshold question. A simple mortgage is made complicated by dividing it into six contractual components, but dividing up the mortgage does not help answer the three important questions:
  —Did the transferor transfer credit risk?
  —Did the transferor transfer interest rate risk?
  —Did the transferor retain an interest in the mortgages?
- The components approach creates the temptation of going down the path of accounting for each individual component and losing sight of the forest for the trees. The approach of accounting for individual components is similar to the wrong turn that the Board took in FASB Statement 77. What is needed is to focus on the transaction as a whole and the risks and benefits of ownership as a whole in deciding whether a sale or a borrowing has taken place. The components have to be looked at in the aggregate in answering the threshold question.
- The paper suggests at one point that perhaps the components are a function of the accounting. I disagree and believe that the components and the ownership of those components is a function of the transaction and the contractual rights of the receivables. Stated differently, the components should be real-world components rather than creations of the accounting, and the accounting should be derived from an analysis of the components rather than vice versa.

Fourth, an additional question that the FASB should consider is whether it is possible to have a sale if it is not possible to identify the investor's ownership other than in terms of cash flows. To illustrate, consider four different types of securitized asset transactions: whole loans, undivided interests, interest-only/principal-only strips, and multiclass passthroughs. In a whole loan transaction, the investors purchase identified receivables. In an undivided interest transaction, the investors own a stated percentage of every loan in the portfolio. In an interest-only/principal-only strip transaction, the investors own all of the interest payments related to the loans in a portfolio or all of the principal payments related to the loans in a portfolio, either one an interest that can be identified at the level of each individual loan. By contrast, in a multiclass passthrough, the investors do not have a defined interest in any individual loan in the portfolio. The investors are entitled to interest income on their investment at a defined rate and are entitled to principal repayments based on some formula. For example, the first principal payments out of the entire pool of loans may be allocated to one class until that class is repaid in full. Only after the class has been paid in full is it possible to go back and determine which individual loans provided the cash flows that were used to pay back the investors in that class. Had the individual debtors behaved differently, the investors would have been paid out by cash flows from different loans. Some accountants, myself included, believe that a multiclass passthrough structure should never be accounted for as a sale because the investors cannot identify an ownership in any individual loan. Their rights can be defined only in terms of how the cash flows from the portfolio will be allocated and are inherently a lender's interest rather than an ownership interest.

Fifth, the FASB should look at the federal income tax rules in this area. The federal income tax rules are not always a good source of guidance for financial reporting, but for securitized assets those rules are driven principally by economic substance defined in terms of which party has the benefits and burdens of ownership similar to the approach Dr. Swieringa suggests. One of the most dispiriting things for an accountant working on many securitized asset transactions treated as sales under Statement 77 is to read the "Federal Income Tax Consequences" section of the prospectus. This is what a typical section, from the prospectus for the first public offering of interests in credit card receivables, said:

> Tax Counsel has advised, for the reasons set forth in its opinion, that the Certificateholders should be treated as having acquired indebtedness of the Bank for Federal and California income tax purposes. Pursuant to the Pooling and Servicing Agreement, the Bank and the Certificate-holders will express their intent that, for Federal and state income tax purposes, the Certificates will be indebtedness of the Bank secured by the Receivables. Each Certificateholder, by the acceptance of its Certificates, will agree to treat the Certificates as indebtedness of the Bank for Federal and state income tax purposes. For certain other purposes, including accounting and regulatory treatment, the Bank will treat the

Pooling and Servicing Agreement as a transfer of ownership of an interest in the Receivables and not a debt obligation of the Bank.

The characterization of the Pooling and Servicing Agreement for Federal and state income tax purposes as creating a debt obligation between the Bank and the Certificateholders rather than a transfer of ownership of an interest in the Receivables depends on the economic substance of the transaction. The form of a transaction, while a relevant factor, is not conclusive evidence of its economic substance. The determination of whether a transfer of property is a sale of property or evidences a loan secured by the transferred property for Federal income tax purposes has been made by the Internal Revenue Service (the "IRS") and the courts on the basis of numerous factors evidencing the economic ownership of the transferred property. A transfer of property has been found to be a sale of the property for Federal income tax purposes when the owner has relinquished substantial incidents of ownership. Among the many factors evidencing the incidents of ownership, the primary factors examined are whether the transferee has assumed the burdens of ownership and acquired the benefits of ownership.

The federal income tax rules in this area are not perfect, but there is an extensive body of regulation and case law focusing on which are the more important incidents of ownership and analyzing when transactions of this sort constitute sales versus collateralized borrowings. The FASB should make use of the insights gained by federal income tax practitioners over the years.

Finally, a minor factual point—the interest retained in a pool of loans by the transferor is not necessarily a subordinated interest as implied by the paper. Sometimes the seller keeps an undivided interest that is equal in seniority to the interest sold. It is possible, although I have not seen examples, for the seller to retain interests that are senior to some of the interests sold to outside investors.

In closing, I would like to summarize my three major points:

- This is an important project to resolve a very troublesome area of financial accounting, and it is good to see the Board beginning to make some progress on these recognition and measurement issues.
- The direction outlined in the paper is fundamentally sound.
- My comments and suggestions today are intended to make the outlined approach more productive and more successful for the Board.

Contract Theoretic Analysis of Off–Balance Sheet Financing

Jim Donegan* and Shyam Sunder**

I. Introduction

This paper analyzes the reporting problems associated with off–balance sheet financing (OBSF) and explores possible resolutions to the controversy that surrounds OBSF and accounting for new types of financial instruments. In the Sections II through IV, we analyze three general issues of financial reporting that are central to an understanding of the disagreements surrounding OBSF: (1) the effect of different perspectives (representational faithfulness, decision usefulness, and contract enforcement or accountability) on financial reporting practices; (2) the duality of stocks and flows, and the attendant problems of classifying contracts for the purpose of financial reporting; and (3) the problem of reporting on statistically or contractually correlated resource flows. After addressing these three theoretical issues, we turn in Section V to examining a common form of off balance sheet financing. We conclude that formulation of intertemporally stable financial reporting standards would be facilitated if (1) contract enforcement considerations were added to the representational faithfulness and decision usefulness perspectives currently used by the Financial Accounting Standards Board (FASB), and (2) the range of financial reporting alternatives considered by the Board were expanded to include expected value reporting on one hand and reporting of contract sets on the other.

II. Financial Reporting Perspectives

Financial reporting practices can be examined from at least three different perspectives: representational faithfulness (RF), decision usefulness (DU), and contract enforcement or accountability. This section reviews the RF and DU viewpoints and provides a more extended treatment of the contracting perspective.

*University of Arizona.

**Carnegie Mellon University.

The first draft of this paper was presented at the Accounting Workshop of the University of Minnesota and at the Conference on Off–Balance Sheet Activities at New York University. In revising the first draft we have benefited from comments received at both presentations, especially those from Jim Ohlson. We alone are responsible for the remaining errors. Additional comments are welcome.

Representational Faithfulness

From the representational faithfulness perspective (FASB [1980], paras. 63–71), the firm is seen as a collection of economic facts; accounting methods are evaluated by their ability to produce numbers and disclosures that approximate these facts as closely as possible. Although alternative formulations of RF are possible, the FASB has interpreted it as a rule of similarity, requiring that a complex accounting event be treated as equivalent to the one simpler event to which it is deemed to have the most in common. As such, some attributes are relied on for the purpose of choosing accounting treatments, and others are suppressed. For example, the equity component of convertible debt can vary from near zero to near one. Yet the accounting treatment of these securities depends on their debt attributes alone. In the presence of uncertainty, the RF criterion, unless further specified, provides little help on selecting a desirable representation of the relevant probability distributions for uncertain cash flows.

Decision Usefulness

The decision usefulness criterion was developed to deal with accounting under uncertainty using statistical decision theory (Churchman and Ackoff [1955]; Davidson and Trueblood [1961]; Demski [1980]; and Demski and Feltham [1976]). Decision usefulness (DU) analysis of accounting examines the value of accounting data, specified by its statistical properties, in assisting investors and managers to make better choices under uncertainty. By attributing a preference function to the decision maker, it is possible to evaluate the degree to which different accounting representations assist the decision maker in arriving at the best feasible outcome. Using the DU criterion permits accountants to assess whether the cost of obtaining and interpreting financial data can be justified by a greater benefit to the decision maker.

The FASB has considered the decision usefulness of accounting information (FASB [1978]) and discussed the trade-off between costs and benefits (FASB [1980], paras. 133–144). However, these statements ignore the fact that many proponents of the DU perspective reject the possibility of rigorously determining the greatest good for the greatest number in setting accounting standards or in any other object of social choice.[1]

---

1. For example, Demski (1974) stated: "[W]e know that no robust concept of optimality exists, unless we admit to a dictatorial imposition" (p. 232).

Contract Enforcement

Under the contract enforcement perspective on accounting, a firm can be seen as a set of contracts among economic agents. Each economic agent—including employees, managers, investors, customers, vendors, government, creditors, and auditors, depending on the context of analysis—is expected to contribute resources and expects to receive resources in exchange. Agents are motivated by their respective preferences for effort, resources, consumption, or other specified factors. Accounting and control system helps implement and enforce the contract set.[2]

Implementation and enforcement of contract sets are complicated by two considerations. First, the contract set is not complete. A complete contract set would specify the rights and obligations of each agent under all contingencies. Even for a simple organization, specifying a complete set of contracts would be a formidable task, considering the large number of possible events on which such relationships may depend. Incomplete contracts necessarily depend on the expectations of participants about what might happen under various contingencies, both anticipated and unanticipated. Successful implementation of contract sets requires that the expectations of the participants are kept sufficiently aligned with one another to minimize the chances of surprise or disappointment and consequent disintegration of the set.

Second, resources vary in the degree to which their stocks and flows can be measured, monitored, or even identified. Measurability of resource contributions and claims of various agents must be reckoned in designing an enforceable contract set. Accounting systems serve these functions—measuring resources and communicating information among the participating agents to minimize the likelihood of too great a divergence between their resource expectations and actual realizations.

When outcomes that are not specifically provided for in the contract set occur, it is useful to have resource allocation devices that will help maintain the stability of the contract set. The participating agents must believe that the *ex post* choice of resource allocation under such circumstances is proximate to what have been agreed on, if considered, *ex ante*. Otherwise the contracting set will be destabilized and may disintegrate in mutual recrimination and distrust. However, this flexibility in the contract set also provides opportunities for various agents, especially the managers who operate the contract set of the firm, to exploit the system to serve their own

---

2. See Ijiri (1975, Chap. 3) on accountability relation and Sunder (1987) on contract enforcement.

ends. In this respect the output of the accounting system is comparable to a public good: Every agent prefers that all other agents cooperate in minimizing the divergence in expectations, while he or she attempts to obtain a maximum allocation of resources for himself or herself. If every agent acted in such a noncooperative fashion, firms would not exist and all participants would be worse off.

The Hierarchy of Perspectives

The degree of representational faithfulness of accounting numbers is an important attribute of accounting information from the DU perspective. In turn, the optimum choice under the DU criterion constitutes steps in the contractual process among agents. These three approaches to accounting can be treated as a hierarchy in which standards development and application can be viewed alternately as a puzzle with an indeterminate solution (representational faithfulness), a game against nature (decision theory), or a game among agents (contract theory). The contracting perspective assumes that solutions to accounting problems will draw on elements from all three levels of this hierarchy.

Both the representational faithfulness and the decision usefulness criteria ignore the action-reaction sequence that occurs between accounting on the one hand and decision making on the other. When decision makers take GAAP as a given, it is often possible for them to act to take advantage of acceptable reporting methods and to make accounting choices that cast their actions in the best possible light. Such motives underlie the design of many new financial instruments and many applications of reporting standards to such instruments and transactions by extension or analogy. Accountants react to such decisions by modifying the accounting standards, or reinterpreting the standards in relationship to newer types of transactions or instruments, and thus present new opportunities for decision makers to modify their behavior. Off—balance sheet financing and financial instruments are prominent, but by no means unique, examples of this action-reaction sequence.

By assuming stationary stochastic processes rather than system evolution, the RF and DU perspectives fail to yield clues about the nature of changes in reporting equilibria. The accountability (or contract theoretic) perspective, on the other hand, approaches the analysis of accounting methods from a systemic perspective: It takes into account the response of all specified agents to the accounting system. Decisions made by various agents are affected by the statistical properties of information available to them, and these decisions in turn affect decisions of others. The questions we must address under this perspective include not only the uncertainty of the accounting environment, and the decision usefulness of data, but also the interaction among decision makers. The contract theoretic perspective may yield accounting methods that are poor in faithfully representing any given parameter of the environment. These methods may even be dominated by other methods that provide information that is statistically more useful for some or every class of decision maker, if considered individually. However, when we consider the ability of various accounting methods to facilitate the execution of contracts among a set of individuals with diverse interests, it may be the case that the best solutions deviate from the solutions generated by the RF and DU criteria.

Having considered the different reporting perspectives, we turn to the second of the issues considered in this paper, the duality of stocks and flows. Although the issue is an old one, we believe the contracting perspective successfully rationalizes existing practices that appear contradictory from the RF viewpoint. This rationale can be extended to yield some insights into the OBSF problem.

III. The Duality of Stocks and Flows and Classification of Contracts

Contracts that constitute a firm specify conditions under which resources are exchanged. It is possible to represent each resource in the form of either a stock or a flow variable. Every stream of flows can be capitalized to its corresponding stock representation through the process of discounting or accumulation; and every stock of resources can be converted into a variety of flow representations. This duality of representation is a fundamental characteristic of all resources.

For some resources (e.g., special-purpose machinery), it is possible to measure the stock with greater accuracy or smaller cost than the corresponding flow, and, therefore, we represent them in terms of stock variables. For other resources (e.g., taxi rides, movie tickets), flow variable representation is more precise or easier to obtain. Sometimes both stock and flow representations are accessible (e.g., rental apartments); and, finally, there are resources for which neither representation is credible (e.g., underground oil reserves, customer goodwill).

Resources for which stock representation is convenient are often said to be ''owned'' by the firm. The label of ownership is only a shorthand expression for two attributes: The specified agent has certain contractual rights to some resources, and these resources have a convenient stock representation. Besides being a label for these attributes, ownership itself has no other implications about the characteristic of resources. Because rights to resources are always contingent on fulfillment of certain conditions, there is no such thing as outright ownership of a resource. The "ownership" of my house, car, and clothes, for example, is simply an expression of certain rights I can expect to enjoy provided that I comply with the mortgage contract with my banker, rules of traffic, and conditions of decency expected by my neighbors.

Given this tentative nature of "ownership," whether or not a resource is recognized in financial statements cannot be determined by asking the question: Does the firm own the resource? To do so would be to beg the question.

Under our current system of financial reporting, articulation between stocks on the balance sheet and flows on the statements of income and changes in cash flow is both incomplete and imperfect; the unavoidable lapses in articulation are critical to understanding the OBSF problem. If we did not require articulation of financial statements, the balance sheet would consist of stock representations of rights and obligations pertaining to resources that can be accurately, conveniently, and promptly measured. Similarly, the income statement would incorporate those resource flows that can be easily and reliably measured. There is no guarantee that the sets of resources whose stocks and flows can be so measured would be identical. In fact, the decades of debate over deferred taxes, replacement cost depreciation, and the income effects of foreign subsidiary translation suggest that we can expect little agreement as to a set of resources whose stocks and flows can readily be represented on financial statements.

Under extant accounting practice, not all resources are recognized as either stocks or flows. Further, some resources are measured as stocks without corresponding flows (e.g., land and pre-1970 goodwill), whereas some flows are measured without related stocks (e.g., research and development outlays and nonfactory wages). Additionally, we attempt to maintain the semblance of articulation by constructing the flow (stock) equivalents of measurable stock (flow) variables (e.g., depreciation of long-term assets in the income statement and capitalization of leases and prepaid costs on the balance sheet). How to construct correspondent variables, and under what conditions it is appropriate to abandon the task of articulation, are questions that lie at the heart of major problems in standardizing accounting practice including OBSF.

In current financial reporting practice, resources included in the financial statements must meet a judgmental threshold of measurability in either their stock or their flow representation. Once a resource enters the balance sheet or the income statement, we try to create a correspondent variable for the other statement through capitalization or amortization. Again, construction of such correspondent variables (e.g., capitalized leases, depreciation) requires that they also meet a judgmental threshold, albeit a lower one, of measurability. In its various pronouncements, the FASB has attempted to use these judgmental thresholds of uncertainty that must exist for application of various accounting treatments. Judgmental thresholds create discontinuities and offer incentives for managers either to alter their judgments about the uncertainty associated with the resource measurement or to redesign contracts to cross the judgmental threshold in the desired direction. For example, a lessor who wishes to recognize the transaction as a sale may understate the risk of default by the lessee. Similarly, a lessee who does not wish to have a liability for lease obligations appear on the balance sheet may adjust the estimated useful life of the leased asset in order to ensure that the lease term is less than the 75 percent threshold. Such efforts to redesign contracts are unlikely to be mitigated by rule makers through adjustments in judgmental thresholds.

We can see two different possibilities for dealing with this problem. Abandonment of articulation between stock and flow statements will solve only the part of the problem that concerns the choice of correspondent variables that depend on judgments about the degree of uncertainty. Moreover, articulation of stock and flow statements is too deeply embedded in the system of double entry bookkeeping to easily be given up now. It may also create more problems than it solves by reducing constraints on managerial behavior.

A second, and more promising, possibility is to abandon the judgmental threshold approach to reporting uncertain events and move toward reporting statistical constructs such as expected values, variances, and correlations. The judgmental threshold approach results in all-or-nothing; the statistical approach will eliminate this discontinuity because small changes in the judgments about uncertainty of a resource flow will result in only small changes in the expected value of the resource. The statistical approach will therefore remove the large incentives that now exist for making even small changes in judgmental uncertainties. On the other hand, a disadvantage of the statistical approach would be that probabilistic judgments will affect *all* resources reported in the financial statements. We return to a discussion of this question in the context of the problem of reporting on correlated resource flows.

IV. Statistical Representation of Correlated Cash Flows

The firm consists of contracts that are interrelated in complex ways. The accounting process deliberately decomposes the complex web of contracts by separately defining small clusters of resource rights and obligations into discrete events. These events are then treated as though they were independent of all others. Complete independence is rarely obtained, but in most cases dependence is sufficiently weak to be ignored for the sake of developing a simple and feasible system of reporting. The problem of accounting for correlated resource flows and of deciding when their collinearity should be recognized in the accounting system is the third basic issue that lies at the root of OBSF.

OBSF as well as defeasance issues can be restated in statistical terms as problems that arise from negative correlation among streams of resources. If correlations were perfect (i.e., if there were no uncertainty), it would be easy to justify OBSF or defeasance.[3] This extreme condition is fulfilled in few cases. The case of zero correlation between resource flows is also easy to handle—record each stream of cash flows separately. How can or should the accountant handle the vast number of cases in which resource streams are significantly but less than perfectly correlated?

In the point-estimation system of financial reporting currently in use, correlation of resource streams may appear to be irrelevant. Since the expected value of the sum or the difference of any two random variables is equal to the sum or difference of their expected values, independent of their correlation, a concern with correlations may appear to be misplaced. Lenders and shareholders, however, are concerned not only with the expected value, but also with the risk of their investments. Since the variance of the sum of random variables depends on their correlation, they play a crucial role in defining the riskiness of investments.

Consider two incremental cash flows represented by random variables x and y. Suppose a firm has existing cash flow z and must decide how to account for these two incremental flows. If x and y have equal expected values and variances and are perfectly negatively correlated, they will cancel each other out under every possible circumstance. Under such conditions, nothing would be gained by supplementing reports of z by reports of x and y. This condition provides the conceptual basis for nonrecognition or defeasance of assets and liabilities. At the other extreme, if x and y had perfect positive correlation, they could be usefully aggregated into one item for the purpose of reporting. Finally, cash flows that are uncorrelated could appear as separate line items in the financial reports. It is possible to create a statistical rationale for such a practice. For example, let us assume that, in the absence of any other information, the readers of financial statements treat the cash flows from each line item in financial statements as essentially independent of one another. The extent of under- or overestimation of the

---

3. In this instance, perfect correlation is perfectly negative.

variance of the sum of the cash flows would be minimized by aggregating cash flows that are highly correlated with one another. Aggregation of positively correlated cash flows will amount to adding them together; aggregation of highly negatively correlated cash flows amounts to netting them out against each other and thus taking them off the balance sheet. The cutoff point for the absolute value of correlation beyond which the items are aggregated could be determined by an appropriately chosen objective function.

The use of classified financial statements provides an approximate solution to the problem of relating cash flows with nonzero correlations. We reinterpret the traditional categories, such as current versus noncurrent assets or selling versus administrative expenses, as qualitative approximations of factors or principal components. Items within a single category presumably would load highest on the same factor. Extending the analogy, ratio analysis can be seen as a search for simple structure, in which moderately correlated resources such as cash, receivables, and inventory are added to form a single numerator. However, the utility of such aggregations is limited since they fail to distinguish common from account-specific variance.

In this section we have examined financial statement recognition and classification from the point of view of correlation between resource flows. From this viewpoint, the joint recognition/classification decision communicates to statement users the expected variance of the resource flows of the firm. Aggregating independent flows and separately reporting highly positively or negatively correlated flows results in a divergence between the expected variance of resources allocated to agents and the actual variance of their realized returns. As discussed in Section II, differences between expectations and realizations attributable to measurement error can destabilize the contract set and may lead to its disintegration.

V. Accounting for Leases

We now apply the insights obtained from the discussion of reporting perspectives, duality of resources, and correlation of resource flows to examine the development and evolution of a perennial OBSF issue—lease accounting. The leasing problem is usually framed as a dichotomous choice between classification of the transaction as a short-term rental or as the purchase of a capital asset. In the RF perspective, choice between these options must be made on the basis of whether the measured stocks and flows of resources correspond closely to the actual quantities. The DU approach considers this choice to be important to the extent specific economic decisions may be influenced by the capitalization/expense decision. From the contracting perspective, the basic issue is the effect of the capitalization/ expense decision on the behavior of various agents, including any action-reaction sequences that are likely to arise and any consequential effects on allocation of the firm's resources.

The Committee on Accounting Procedure was the first authoritative body to consider the issue of the accounting treatment for lease contracts that were installment purchases in all material respects (AICPA [1949]). Transfer of ownership at the end of the lease term and the existence of bargain purchase options were identified by the Committee as conditions that create a presumption of purchase equivalence. The cash flows associated with these leased assets were perfectly positively correlated with traditionally acquired fixed assets; the related obligations were equally well correlated with the corresponding long-term debt. Since the RF perspective treats transactions as being either perfectly correlated with, or else completely independent of, all other transactions, it provided adequate guidance for classifying such leases.

As the leasing industry evolved, contracts containing increasingly complex rules for determining resource inputs and allocations proliferated. To some degree this evolution reflected an action-reaction sequence in which managers sought the most advantageous (to them) contracts obtainable under the prevailing accounting rules. Standardized lease contracts were replaced by leases that were increasingly tailored to the unique needs of individual lessors and lessees. As lease contracts proliferated to populate the continuum from full to minimal transfer of property rights, the RF perspective no longer yielded a categorization that captured the differences in statistical correlation between financial leases and purchases. Economic agents (particularly debtors and shareholders) could no longer form reasonably precise expectations as to the expected variance of resource flows. This diffusion of expectations represents a disintegrative force promoting hostile gaming among economic agents.

The DU perspective provided the rationale for the increasingly complex leasing standards issued by the Accounting Principles Board following ARB 38 in 1949. To reflect the inadequacy of dichotomous classification, APB Opinions 5, 7, and 31 (AICPA [1964, 1966, 1973]) stressed appropriate disclosures to inform users of the distortions imposed by the traditional taxonomy and thereby improve signal fineness. The use of multiple objective tests for purchase equivalence embodied in SFAS 13 (FASB [1976]) can be viewed as a DU-based attempt to reduce the noisiness of lease reporting.

These standards paid little attention to the potential responses of the agents whose attempts to maximize their own welfare started the leasing game. Noncooperative behavior has dominated the evolution of lease accounting, and some standards encourage such behavior. Managers have attempted, apparently with some success, to classify financial leases as operating rentals. From the shareholders' and bondholders' point of view, such attempts lead to a divergence between expected and actual resource allocations. In reaction, share and bond prices may be bid down to reflect the diffusion in expectations created by self-serving management; compensation plans may be rewritten to place bounds on the compensation effects of managerial discretion; or more auditing may be demanded. Any of these outcomes can lead to a weakening of the contracting set that we call the firm. Such a result is ultimately inferior for managers as well as for other participating agents.

The tailing off of new lease standards appears to be due to the FASB's having imposed sufficient costs on avoiding capitalization as to exceed marginal benefits. This solution imposes costs on practically all agents. However, it appears that innovative management has recouped lost momentum by shifting to other types of financial instruments or inventing new ones.

The contracting perspective suggests a simple conceptual solution to the spiral in which each new standard creates new loopholes. If the motives of, and opportunities available to, managers can be inferred *ex ante,* we could construct a standards-setting process that anticipates self-interested accounting choice. A major weakness of current accounting for financial instruments is the all-or-nothing approach to classification. As long as leases are dichotomously categorized as assets or expenses, self-serving choice will be encouraged. The existence of arbitrary break points, such as the 90 percent rule, exacerbate the problem. Even if the rule is applied by disinterested parties, it can lead to dramatically different treatments of transactions that have only minute differences in the neighborhood of break points (such as 90 percent value or 75 percent service life).

For example, consider two firms (A and B) each with $100 of debt and equity (exclusive of capitalized lease obligations). Both have a debt-equity ratio (D/E) of 1. If A enters into a capital lease valued at 80 percent of the leased asset's FMV of $100, A's D/E will remain unchanged. If B enters into a similar lease except that the guaranteed payments are equal to 90 percent of FMV, B's new D/E will be 1.9. Unsurprisingly, different means (1.45 versus 1.85) are obtained depending on whether the SFAS 13 criterion or expected value rules are applied. Of greater interest is the difference in variance. SFAS 13 yields a variance of 0.5, whereas the variance based on expected value is 0.005. If we assume a more reasonable distribution of expected values (e.g., D/E increasing in intervals of 0.05 from 0.55 to 1.0 for ten firms.), the differences in variance remains at over 100 percent (0.048 as opposed to 0.023).[4]

Thus, the discontinuity of results can be reduced (with corresponding reduction in the incentives for manipulation) by reporting expected values instead. However, reporting of expected values may induce managers to engage in a different kind of manipulation—the manipulation of subjective probabilities. Further investigation would be necessary to determine whether such substitution is a dominant solution.

VI. Conclusions

OBSF may be described generally as netting out a pair of negatively correlated resources against each other to omit both from a firm's balance sheet. Such treatment would be fully justified if the negative correlation were perfect. In practice, perfect correlation is rarely achieved and justification for off–balance sheet treatment depends on the degree of imperfection. Since the off–balance sheet threshold is essentially a subjective judgment about negative correlation, the current regulatory stance offers managers an opportunity to push this threshold toward zero.

We have considered three major issues concerning off–balance sheet financing. Three perspectives on financial reporting—representative faithfulness, decision usefulness, and contract theoretic—have a hierarchical relationship to one another. Consideration of RF enters into individual decisions and individual decisions in turn constitute moves in a game among economic agents. The FASB appears to have stopped short of taking this last step in setting accounting standards. The history of leasing and lease accounting is an example of the instability that results from a failure to recognize the gaming nature of the accounting environment.

If intertemporal stability of accounting standards were regarded as a desirable attribute of the accounting environment, contract theory suggests that the regulators might want to strive for accounting rules that define a game whose Nash equilibrium is acceptable to them as an outcome. Nash equilibrium of a game describes those set(s) of individual strategies or decision rules that, if followed by all participants, yield outcome(s) that cannot be improved on by any one of the participants through unilateral defection. Empirical work in game theory suggests that outcomes of most

---

4. This distribution is arrived at by assuming that all firms have $100 of debt and $200 of equity exclusive of lease activity. The calculated variances are obtained by assuming that the leases have expected values ranging from $10 to $100 in $10 increments.

games can be predicted accurately by assuming that agents choose Nash decision rules. In other words, Nash equilibrium is a good descriptive model of how people behave in interactive economic environments. Investors, managers, auditors, and other agents play a financial reporting game whose rules are defined, in part, by the Securities and Exchange Commission and the FASB. In order to assess the consequences of proposed regulatory actions, it is reasonable for them to assume that outcomes will lie with the set of Nash equilibria of the game.

We have no algorithm for determining Nash equilibria for the complex game of financial reporting. But then, there is no general algorithm for arriving at accounting rules that fulfill the RF and DU criteria either. Yet the consideration of these criteria helps regulators frame the debate and narrow down the range of choices. The concept of Nash equilibrium still provides a useful guideline for the rule makers to inform themselves of the consequences of their proposed actions. If an accounting standard is based on assuming a behavior on the part of some individuals that does not appear to be in the best interest of the individuals, there is a good chance that such an assessment of consequences may prove to be incorrect.

It may be fruitful to undertake the exercise of constructing action-re-action sequences for proposed rules. Accounting rules that fulfill the RF or DU criteria can be the starting points of such exercises. We may end up adopting accounting rules that are not the best by RF and DU standards but that constitute achievable, enforceable, and stable solutions in our imperfect world.

After considering the duality of stocks and flows, we conclude that it is not possible to construct perfectly articulated balance sheet and income/cash flow statements. Perfect articulation would force inclusion of highly uncertain correspondent variables in financial statements. On the other hand, abandoning articulation completely is not feasible either. As firms enter into increasingly complex contractual arrangements, a feasible solution is to begin to experiment with extended disclosure of terms of contracts in the financial reports. The cost of this move—more pages and fine print—is not welcome in itself. But that is the choice made—not by accountants, but by the managers who design complex contracts.

Finally, a consideration of the statistical attributes of resource flows and of contracts (off-balance sheet financing as well as other financial instruments) leads us to suggest that the rule makers might consider proposing (1) explicitly probabilistic reporting of financial estimates in instances where frequency data from the past can be used to support such reports and (2) explicit statistical criteria for recognition and defeasance of assets and liabilities under such circumstances. Under the current system, all probabilities (with the exception with respect to estimated liabilities) as well as correlations must be reduced to either zero or one. This practice encourages game playing on the part of managers because small changes in the terms of contracts in the neighborhood threshold values can have large effects on the appearance of financial statements. Expected value reporting will eliminate this discontinuity, so that small changes in the terms of contracts will have only small effects on the appearances of financial statements and will thus discourage the sort of behavior that has created the crisis of accounting for off–balance sheet financing and financial instruments.

REFERENCES

American Institute of Certified Public Accountants, Committee on Accounting Procedure. Accounting Research Bulletin No. 38, *Disclosure of Long-Term Leases in Financial Statements of Lessees* (AICPA, 1949).

———. Accounting Principles Board. Opinion No. 5, *Reporting of Leases in Financial Statements of Lessees* (AICPA, 1964).

———. Accounting Principles Board. Opinion No. 7, *Accounting for Leases in Financial Statements of Lessors* (AICPA, 1966).

———. Accounting Principles Board. Opinion No. 31, *Disclosure of Lease Commitments by Lessees* (AICPA, 1973).

Churchman, D. West, and Ackoff, Russell L. "Operational Accounting and Operations Research." *Journal of Accounting* (February 1955), pp. 33–39.

Davidson, H. Justin, and Trueblood, Robert M. "Accounting for Decision Making." *The Accounting Review* 36 (October 1961), pp. 577–582.

Demski, Joel. "Choice among Financial Reporting Alternatives." *The Accounting Review* 49 (April 1974), pp. 221–232.

———. *Information Analysis* (Addison-Wesley, 1980).

Demski, Joel, and Gerald Feltham. *Cost Determination: A Conceptual Approach* (Iowa State University, 1976).

Financial Accounting Standards Board. Statement No. 12, *Accounting for Certain Marketable Securities* (FASB, 1975).

———. Statement No. 13, *Accounting for Leases* (FASB, 1976).

———. Concepts Statement No. 1, *Objectives of Financial Reporting by Business Enterprises* (FASB, 1978).

———. Concepts Statement No. 2, *Qualitative Characteristics of Accounting Information* (FASB, 1980).

———. Statement No. 77, *Receivables Sold with Recourse* (FASB, 1983).

Ijiri, Yuji. *Theory of Accounting Measurement*. Studies in Accounting Measurement No. 10 (American Accounting Association, 1975).

Sunder, Shyam. "A Contract Theory of Accounting and Control in Organizations." (University of Minnesota, 1987).

The Use of Off–Balance Sheet Financing to Circumvent Financial Covenant Restrictions

Samir El-Gazzar,* Steven Lilien,** and Victor Pastena**

This paper explores whether the use of off balance sheet financing (OBSF) techniques such as operating lease accounting can loosen potentially binding covenant constraints. Currently, there is little evidence on the extent of tailoring of covenant definitions in debt agreements. Exposition of the details of lending agreements should facilitate an understanding of the ability of managers to avoid the consequences of financial covenant violations.

The operating method of accounting for leases is a form of OBSF because debt is not recognized for balance sheet purposes in spite of the lessee's obligation to make lease payments. The operating method also allows lessees with growing activities to report higher income. In contrast, lease capitalization puts a lease liability on the balance sheet and lessees who capitalize are likely to report high interest expenses early in the lease life.

This research examines accounting definitions of a sample of private debt covenants negotiated by firms with substantial amounts of lease OBSF and explores the potential for mitigation of binding constraints by using OBSF. In particular, this study probes whether the choice of the operating method of lease accounting can mitigate covenant constraints concerning (1) dividend payments, (2) additional debt, (3) production/investment decisions, and (4) payout decisions.

Also, this study revisits the academic conflict on whether managerial choices such as the use of OBSF can loosen binding covenant constraints. Many prior studies assume that financial contracts use a firm's GAAP (generally accepted accounting principles) accounting to calculate covenant-based financial ratios; thus, managers' GAAP choices *will affect* the tightness of financial covenant constraints. For example, Abdel-khalik [1], El-Gazzar, Lilien, and Pastena [2], and Imhoff and Thomas [3] argue that one consequence of regulatory limitations on using operating method lease accounting was to place formerly operating method lessees closer to violation of debt covenants.

*Rutgers University.
**Baruch College of CUNY.

In contrast, Leftwich [4] and Holthausen and Leftwich [5] argue that often private debt covenants specify non-GAAP accounting for purposes of determining financial ratios in debt covenants; and Leftwich reports that private financial covenants typically require the capitalization method that places leasing debt on the balance sheet. If the details of covenant accounting specified within the contract and covenant accounting rules are independent of managers' GAAP choices, managerial use of OBSF for leases *will not affect* the tightness of financial covenant constraints.

To deal with the issue of whether managers' GAAP choices matter, this study provides numerical evidence on covenant restrictions, the accounting definitions used within covenants, and the interaction between financial covenants and accounting definitions in those covenants. The interactions between covenants and definitions within covenants provide a basis for conclusions concerning the ability of managerial actions to circumvent potential covenant restrictions.

Prior Research and the Role of the Current Study

Based on the American Bar Association's *Commentaries on Debentures,* Leftwich [4] and Smith and Warner [6] provide descriptions of the types of financial covenant constraints and accompanying definitions. *Commentaries,* is a compilation of typical covenants in lending agreements by the American Bar Association.

Leftwich supplements *Commentaries,* with a small sample of private debt contracts of insurance companies. He reports that some accounting measurements were entirely outside GAAP, others were partially consistent with GAAP, and others were entirely consistent with GAAP. As a deviation from GAAP for covenant purposes, Leftwich observes that leases are capitalized in private debt contracts, even though current GAAP offered considerable procedural flexibility in accounting for leases. These findings imply that (1) negotiations on terms of debt agreements reduce the conflict between lenders and stockholders, and (2) incentives of managers to select those methods under GAAP that ease contractual restrictions may not be as great as previously implied in the "agency" literature.

However, the use of *Commentaries* rather than actual contracts to draw inferences on the frequency of non-GAAP accounting in debt covenants is subject to criticism. Thornton and Bryant [7] argue, "The frequent occurrence of TAP (tailored accounting principles) in *Commentaries on Debentures* does not necessarily indicate the prevalence of TAP in actual bond covenants, since not all covenants necessarily use boilerplate."

Thornton and Bryant use a sample of actual Canadian agreements to explore covenant-based lease accounting. In contrast to Leftwich, Thornton and Bryant do not find substantial covenant-based tailoring of lease accounting. This implies that Canadian firms might use OBSF (operating leases) to circumvent potential covenant restrictions.

As suggested in Thornton and Bryant, the current paper uses actual debt covenants rather than *Commentaries* to measure the extent of non-GAAP accounting. However, a sample of American rather than Canadian covenants is utilized. The Leftwich assertion that lenders significantly tailor definitions within financial covenants is in conflict with the debt hypothesis of El-Gazzar et al. They hypothesize that one motivation for managers' use of the operating method for lease accounting is to alleviate the tightness of financial covenant constraints. Evidence reported here attempts to resolve this conflict.

The Analysis of Actual Financial Covenants

Sample

The current study analyzes the debt contracts negotiated by intensive lessees prior to 1976 to determine whether lessees were able to use OBSF to mitigate financial constraints. El-Gazzar et al. point out that intensive lessees are likely to be high-debt firms whose covenant constraints are negotiated to protect the lenders. Thus, the sample is not random, but rather one that should reflect the results of contracting by knowledgeable lenders and borrowers.

An analysis of *Accounting Trends and Techniques* indicates that 113 firms treated all their leases as operating leases prior to FASB Statement No. 13 and were forced to account for those leases as capital leases under that Statement. Since these intensive lessees did not report lease debt on their financial statements until forced to by Statement 13, these lessees represent a group of firms that chose to use OBSF despite leasing activities having the economic characteristics of debt under the criteria of Statement 13.

The Form 10-Ks for 1970 through 1981 of these formerly operating method lessees were examined to obtain suitable financial agreements. Although firms were not required to include private lending agreements as part of annual report information, some firms incorporated them into their Form 10-Ks when they complied with new disclosure requirements of the SEC's Integrated Disclosure System in 1980 and 1981. Private agreements disclosed along with Form 10-Ks are the basis of the current sample.

As a result of this analysis of lessees' Form 10-Ks, forty-three private lending agreements negotiated before 1977 were found to be incorporated as exhibits to their Form 10-Ks. Table 1 lists the forty-three covenants constituting the sample. Other firms disclosed the private contracts as amendments to the less-accessible Forms 8-K and 10-Q which are not available at SEC regional offices.

The financial statements in the year of change to lease capitalization provide evidence on how the operating method decreases debt and increases income. On average, the debt to equity ratio increases 32 percent and income decreases 6 percent as a result of these lessees' being forced to switch to lease capitalization by Statement 13.

General Restrictions on Managerial Actions

Using the framework provided by Smith and Warner, we categorize the financial covenants into those limiting dividend payments, additional leverage, the firm's production/investment policies, and payoff patterns. Table 2 enumerates the covenants that had covenant-based restrictions.

A total of thirty-seven of the forty-three lending agreements place restrictions on payment of dividends, thirty-one on additional debt, thirty-three on production/investment, and fourteen on payoff patterns. Some lending agreements place more than one financial-based restriction in any given category. These numbers are consistent with the discussion in Smith and Warner.

Can Dividend Restrictions Be Avoided?

Table 3 indicates that the lending agreements contain forty-five different covenant-based dividend constraints. Consistent with Tighe [8], the typical dividend constraints either (1) totally forbid any declaration of dividends, (2) allow a declaration if some key ratio is met, or (3) permit declaration based on achieving a specified income level. Fifty-eight percent of the covenants contain a constraint based on cumulative profitability and additional equity sales after the date of the agreement. Another 9 percent of covenants require firms to maintain a minimum level of net worth before any dividend payments are permitted, and 9 percent forbid any distribution. The ratio of net worth to funded debt is used in four of the lending agreements.

Most covenants with dividends-based restrictions use cumulative profitability subsequent to the date of debt issuance. The majority of the remaining covenants use a net worth measure to restrict dividend payments.

TABLE 1

Sample of 43 Covenants

Company	Date
American Air Filter	3/1/70
American Brands	5/1/70
American Brands	9/1/74
American Brands	3/1/75
AMFAC	1976
AMFAC	6/22/76
Arden-Mayfair	1976
Arvin Mayfair	9/1/76
Burroughs	6/1/67
Burroughs	4/1/70
Burroughs	1963
Deere & Co.	1958
Evans Products	6/1/73
Evans Products	12/31/74
Evans Products	1976
Frontier Airlines	3/1/67
Frontier Airlines	10/15/67
Frontier Airlines	12/15/72
GAF Corp.	4/7/76
Grand Union	10/1/71
Grand Union	12/1/75
Great Western	1/26/72
Harnischfeger Corp.	2/1/76
Hawaiian Airlines	1976
HJ Heinz	4/59
HJ Heinz	12/22/67
HJ Heinz	8/1/72
Island Creek	12/15/75
JC Penney	7/15/70
JP Stevens	4/1/65
Memorex Corp.	4/1/70
National Presto	1960
Pepsico	12/22/72
Jet Air Leasing	3/19/75
SCM Corp.	1968
Sears & Roebuck	1970
Sherwin Williams	11/15/76
Tenneco	5/1/75
Insilco	6/5/75
Ward Foods	3/10/75
West Point Pepperell	10/15/75
West Point Pepperell	12/1/76
Wilson Sporting Goods	10/15/68

Only four covenants consider debt levels in the dividend limitation formula. Since covenants use cumulative profitability and net worth to limit dividends, the ability of managers to mitigate the effects of dividend constraints depends on income and net worth covenant definitions.

TABLE 2

General Constraints for the 43 Covenants

Type of General Constraint	No. of Covenants	% Based on 43 Covenants
Dividend restrictions	37	86
Production and investment restrictions	33	76
Restrictions on additional debt	31	72
Payoff pattern	14	33

Covenant Definitions of Income

Table 4 examines income definitions utilized within covenants containing a dividend restriction based on either cumulative profitability, net worth to funded debt, or net worth as a constant. For the twenty-six covenants constraining dividends based on cumulative profitability, *the starting point is GAAP-based income*. The cumulative profitability equation is then tailored in five instances to exclude preacquisition retained earnings picked up under pooling. In seven instances the excess of income under the equity method above dividends received for investments carried under the equity method is disallowed for covenant purposes. Two covenants tailor for acquisition-related goodwill.

The other modifications to GAAP include a depreciation adjustment, an adjustment for net-of-tax interest on debentures, an adjustment for a discount on a mortgage, an adjustment for income reported by a subsidiary, and an

TABLE 3

Constraints on Dividends

Form of Limitation	No. of Covenants*	% Based on 43 Covenants
Constant plus cumulative income from covenant date plus cash proceeds from stock sales	26	58
Net worth as a constant	7	16
Net worth/funded debt	4	9
No dividends can be declared during term of loan	4	9
Other	4	9
Total	45	

Other:
1. Working capital restrictions.
2. No forgiveness of a specified amount of indebtedness.
3. No repurchase of stock or subordinated indebtedness.
4. Unencumbered assets must be below a percentage of liabilities and capitalized rentals.

*More than one per lending agreement can exist.

TABLE 4

Income Definitions in Lending Agreements Containing a Dividend Constraint

Adjusted for the Following:

Company	GAAP Income	Depreciation	Instant Earnings Under Poolings	Equity Method Income	Goodwill	Gains on Disposition of Capital Assets	Other
American Air Filter	X		X	X	X		
AMFAC	X						
Arden Mayfair	X						X
Arvin Industries	X			X			
Burroughs (6/1/67)	X			X			
Burroughs (1963)	X			X			
Evans Products (6/73)	X			X			
Evans Products (12/74)	X					X	
Frontier Airlines (3/67)	X						
Frontier Airlines (10/67)	X						
GAF Corp.	X						X
Grand Union (10/71)	X						X
Grand Union (12/75)	X						
H.J. Heinz (4/59)	X		X				
H.J. Heinz (12/67)	X		X				
H.J. Heinz (8/72)	X		X				
JC Penney	X						X
JP Stevens	X		X				
Memorex							X
Pepsico	X						
SCM	X			X			
Tenneco	X	X					
Insilco	X						
West Point Pepperell (75)							X
West Point Pepperell (76)	X			X	X	X	
Wilson Sporting Goods	X						
Total	24	1	5	7	2	2	6

Other Modifications to GAAP Income:
Arden Mayfair—Net of tax interest on debentures removed.
GAF—Adjustment for subsidiary income.
Grand Union—Adjustment for consolidated fixed charges.
JC Penney—Adjustment for discount on mortgages.
Memorex—No definition of income provided.
West Point Pepperell (10/15/75)—No definition of income provided.

adjustment for consolidated fixed charges. Essentially, there are no adjustments for mandated or voluntary changes made by any firm. Two of the covenants did not define income.

For the four covenants with dividend constraints based on the ratio of net worth to funded debt, one covenant is based entirely on GAAP income and another adjusts GAAP income for the depreciation method used by the firm. Two covenants offer no definition of income at all. The four covenants that constrain dividend payments based on net worth do not contain any income definition. The three others are based entirely on GAAP except for one covenant that tailors for income picked up under the equity method.

None of the income definitions observed in this section impute interest expense on OBSF. Also, GAAP accounting method choices have considerable impact on the amount of dividends that can be paid, since lenders in general do not appear to tailor those income numbers. This general finding holds true regardless of whether the dividend constraints are based on an equation, constant amount, or ratio.

Definition of Net Worth

This subsection explores whether dividend restriction covenants adjust for OBSF in their definitions of net worth. Table 5 examines definitions of net worth utilized within the twenty-two covenants that use the concept of net worth. Eighteen covenants specifically define net worth; four covenants do not. Tighe indicates that lenders are reluctant to specifically define covenants since that leads to drafting problems and also requires firms to maintain an "additional set of books." Accordingly, the absence of a specific definition probably means the ratios and accompanying financial statements are based on practice (i.e., the common guidelines and rules under GAAP).

Table 5 summarizes the major ways in which net worth is tailored and shows that sixteen of the twenty-two covenants utilizing ratio-based restrictions either specifically indicate GAAP or require no additional tailoring of the definition of net worth. Table 6 illustrates adjustments to the definition of net worth for intangibles assets, deferred taxes, subordinated debt, contingency reserves, and the effects of foreign currency transactions. Only one agreement deals with impact of accounting changes on net worth.

As in the case of covenant-based income definitions, there is no attempt to adjust the definition of net worth to adjust for OBSF. In the case of the four dividend restrictions that utilize funded debt, it will be shown later that only two of these adjust for off-balance sheet leasing. Thus, on a total of forty-five covenant restrictions on dividends by thirty-seven firms, only two

TABLE 5

Definitions of Net Worth (Shareholders' Equity)

Covenant-Based Definition of Net Worth	No. of Covenants	% Based on 22
GAAP shareholders' equity (SE)	8	36.0
GAAP SE less intangible assets	3	14.0
GAAP SE excluding the effects of foreign currency adjustments	1	4.5
GAA book value less liabilities and reserves for contingencies	1	4.5
GAAP SE plus deferred taxes	1	4.5
GAAP SE plus subordinated debentures	1	4.5
GAAP SE plus subordinated debt less intangibles less some deferred taxes	1	4.5
GAAP SE adjusted for accounting changes plus subordinated debt plus minority interest	1	4.5
Total covenants that defined SE	17	77.0
Covenants that do not define SE (GAAP assumed)	5	23.0

consider OBSF. This evidence indicates that, *managers can circumvent covenant dividend restrictions through OBSF*.

Can Restrictions on Additional Debt Be Avoided?

Table 7 shows that there are fifty-two instances where the borrower is restricted from incurring additional debt based on financial covenant constraints. Whereas thirteen constraints simply limit the level of secured debt, another thirteen of the covenants are either written in terms of the debt to equity ratio or the ratio of funded debt to net worth. Another eight constraints (19 percent) are based on net tangible assets to funded debt. Surprisingly,

TABLE 6

Summary of Major Modifications of GAAP SE

Modification	No. of Covenants*	% Based on 22
None or not defined	12	55
Subtract intangible assets	4	18
Adjust for subordinated debt	3	14
Eliminate foreign currency	1	5
Subtract contingency reserve	1	5
Adjust deferred taxes	2	10
Adjust for voluntary accounting change	1	5
Adjust for minority interest	1	5
Total	25	

*Covenant can have more than one modification.

TABLE 7

Constraints on Additional Debt

Definition of Constraints	No. of Covenants	% Based on 43 Covenants
Debt/equity	7	16
Funded debt/net worth	6	14
Net tangible assets/funded debt	8	19
General limits on secured debt	13	30
Income-based restriction	1	2
Interest coverage	4	9
Set dollar limit	1	2
Other	12	28

Other includes:
   1. Analyze whether leasing of assets causes funded debt constraint.
   2. No new funded debt or preferred stock.
   3. Limit based on ratio debt + subordinated debt + real estate/net worth.
   4. No new funded debt unless existing funded debt is redeemed.
   5. No new leases as lessee.
   6. Contingent liabilities should not exceed 1/3 of net worth and subordinated debt should not exceed 1/10 of net worth.
   7. Consolidated funded debt ≤ 35% total capitalized and leasing is not to exceed specified % sales. Total capitalized is defined as net tangible assets plus funded debt.
   8. No new funded debt if exempted indebtedness exceeds 5% shareholders' equity. Exempted indebtedness is debt maturing within 1 year + funded debt + attributable debt (rental operations).
   9. Net tangible assets/(funded debt + preferred stock).
   10. Funded debt must not exceed 35% of total capitalization.
   11. Funded debt may not exceed 70% of (shareholders' equity + funded debt − intangibles).

only four covenants limit debt based on an interest coverage ratio. The covenants in the other category are very customized and do not display any common pattern.

A determination of whether managers can circumvent these potentially binding covenant restrictions depends on the specifics of the definitions of debt, funded debt, and net tangible assets for covenant purposes. The definitions of these terms are illustrated in the next subsection.

Covenant-Based Definitions of Debt, Funded Debt, and Net Tangible Assets

As indicated in Table 7, fifty-two different additional debt restrictions are incorporated in the forty-three covenants. Frequently, this is accomplished by requiring firms to maintain specific debt to net worth or net tangible assets ratios. Usually debt is compared to net worth and funded debt is compared to net tangible assets.

Table 8 provides definitions of debt utilized within the twenty-two covenants that use debt in a ratio that restricts managerial actions; the table shows that ten financial covenant restrictions (46 percent) do not define debt and two require debt to be measured under GAAP. Essentially, 60 percent

TABLE 8

Covenant-Based Definitions of Debt for 22 Firms Having a Leverage Constraint

Type of Covenant Definition	No. of Firms	% Based on 22 Firms
Unmodified GAAP	3	13.5
GAAP debt plus guarantees, mortgages, or liens	3	13.5
GAAP debt plus capital leases	2	9.0
All interest-bearing debt but excluding leases plus guarantees	3	13.5
GAAP current debt plus sinking fund obligations	1	4.5
Total covenants defining debt in covenants	12	54.0
Covenants not defining debt	10	46.0

of the agreements do not tailor the calculation of debt for either leases or any other accounting item.

In two instances the financial-based restrictions require the inclusion of capital leases, even though the firms chose to use their discretion under GAAP to structure leases as operating leases. Two covenants specifically exclude all leases, consistent with the GAAP accounting of firms. Other specific tailorings of debt include guarantees, liens, and sinking fund commitments.

Table 9 provides definitions of funded debt utilized in twenty-two lending agreements containing financial covenant restrictions on additional debt. Fourteen covenants (64 percent) either define funded debt as GAAP debt maturing in more than one year or do not provide a definition within the covenant. Seven covenants (32 percent) tailor the definition of debt to include guarantees of the debt of subsidiaries or other corporations. Only two covenants (9 percent) define leases as long-term debt, and an additional two specifically exclude leases.

Although two covenants include the present value of lease payments in

TABLE 9

Covenant Definitions of Funded Debt

Covenant Definition	No. of Cases	% Based on 22 Cases
GAAP debt maturing in more than one year	5	23
GAAP debt maturing in more than one year plus guarantees for which company is liable	7	30
GAAP debt maturing after one year plus some leases	2	9
Total defining funded debt	14	62
Cases not defining funded debt (GAAP presumed)	8	37

TABLE 10

Covenant-Based Definitions of Net Tangible Assets

Definitions of Net Tangible Assets	No. of Firms	% Based on 22 Firms
All GAAP assets less goodwill, patents, other intangibles, unamortized debt discounts, and restricted investments	3	13.5
All GAAP assets less (1) liabilities reserves (except for funded debt, retained earnings, and deferred taxes), (2) write-up of assets above cost, (3) goodwill and other intangibles, and (4) investments, loans, and advances to nonaffiliates	4	18.0
GAAP asset net of intangibles plus capitalized leases reduced by liabilities (except funded debt)	1	4.5
Total providing definitions of net tangible assets	8	36.0
Total not defining net tangible assets	14	64.0

the debt calculation, most agreements for these leasing-intensive firms do not include the present value of operating leases as debt. These observations are in conflict with Leftwich, who reports that negotiated accounting rules in most agreements require capitalization of leases.

Table 10 provides definitions of net tangible assets as utilized in the twenty-two covenants with financial-based constraints on additional debt. Fourteen (64 percent) of the covenants do not specifically define net tangible assets and apparently are calculated under GAAP. Three covenants (13 percent) define net tangible assets as assets reduced by certain intangibles. Another four covenants (17 percent) define net tangible assets as assets reduced by all liabilities exclusive of deferred taxes and funded debt and additionally reduced by certain intangibles. Only one covenant increases net tangible assets for capitalized leases.

The weight of the evidence provided in Tables 7 through 10 indicates that firms were able to circumvent covenant-based restrictions on additional debt by using operating leases. For the twenty-two lending agreements that used debt in financial-based leverage constraints, Table 8 reports only two required capitalization of operating leases. In fact, three agreements specifically exclude leases from debt, conforming with the choice of the operating method for financial reporting.

The analysis of the funded debt and net tangible assets definition also supports the general conclusions that *firms' use of OBSF can circumvent debt restrictions*. Only two of twenty-two covenants that use funded debt require the capitalization of leases. Similarly, only one of the covenants that use net tangible assets requires lease capitalization.

TABLE 11

Constraints on Production and Investment

Nature of Constraints	No. of Covenants	% Based on 43 Covenants
Merger or acquisition	16	37
Disposition of certain assets	13	30
Insufficiency of working capital	14	33
Sale and leaseback	13	30
Additional rentals	6	14
Additional investments	6	14
Insufficiency of earnings	3	7
Other	7	16

Can Production, Investment, and Payout Restrictions Be Avoided?

Table 11 lists the restrictions on production and investment and Table 12 lists the restrictions on payout. Tighe indicates that these production and investment restrictions are designed to achieve an asset-liability mix and to ensure continued existence of the borrower, whereas constraints on payoff patterns ensure priorities on repayments. Both types of restrictions are frequently referred to as negative covenants because they prohibit certain, specified actions.

Generally, production and investment constraints are not accounting-based but include limits on mergers and acquisitions, additional rentals, additional investments, sale and leaseback, and disposition of assets. However, fourteen production and investment constraints require designated levels of working capital, and three are based on earnings or net worth. Negative payoff covenants restrict the issuance of secured debt, define a priority of

TABLE 12

Restrictions on Payoff Pattern

Type of Payoff Restriction	# of Covenants	% Based on 43 Covenants
Mandatory sinking fund	3	7
Priority of claims on income	4	9
Restrictions on additional secured debt	13	30
Interest on subordinate debt is contingent on earnings	1	2
Restrictions on proceeds from disposal of assets	1	2
Restrictions on securing debt based on ratios of net tangible assets to funded debt and senior debt	1	1

claims, and require sinking funds for debt repayment. Table 12 indicates that payoff patterns are not enforced with accounting-based ratios.

Table 11 indicates that lenders are aware of the leasing activities of their borrowers. The production and investment restrictions show that thirteen agreements prohibit sales and leasebacks that under GAAP allow an accounting profit but create an OBSF liability. Another six agreements prohibit additional rentals, a prohibition that implicitly acknowledges that these rentals were tantamount to additional debt. A total of thirteen of the payout restrictions prohibit additional secured debt. It seems that *lenders did protect themselves against extensive OBSF in the production, investment, and payout restrictions* despite the debtors' ability to circumvent most new debt and dividend restrictions by using OBSF.

Conclusions

This study quantifies the Smith and Warner findings that covenants place restrictions on dividends, additional debt, production and investment decisions, and the pattern of payoffs. It reports that accounting-based constraints are used primarily to restrict managers' discretion to pay future payments or incur additional debt. Dividend restrictions depend primarily on net income and net worth. A variety of leverage ratios including debt to equity and net tangible assets to funded debt are used to restrict a manager's ability to issue additional debt.

The evidence presented here supports the contention that managerial decisions such as using OBSF are able to modify covenant-based restrictions. Most prior research in the area of accounting choice seems justified in the general assumption that accounting choices under GAAP affects covenant-based constraints.

In attempting to understand financial covenants, the current evidence indicates a need for caution when relying on *Commentaries on Indentures* to identify how agreements are tailored because it does not report tailoring of GAAP by frequency of occurrence. Although some lending agreements are tailored to the specific circumstances of the debtor, the current results do not indicate any consistency in the pattern of tailoring across lending agreements.

Modifications to GAAP net income are minimal except in the areas of intangibles, pooling, and equity method accounting. With the exception of guarantees, modifications to debt also are minimal. The current results do not indicate that lending agreements require capitalization of leases. In fact, lending agreements show minimal tailoring of GAAP numbers to compensate for OBSF.

REFERENCES

A. R. Abdel-khalik. *Economic Effects on Leases of FASB Statement No. 13* (1971).

S. El-Gazzar, S. Lilien, and V. Pastena. "Accounting for Leases by Lessees. *Journal of Accounting and Economics* (1986), pp. 217–237.

E. Imhoff and S. Thomas. "Accounting Standards and Firm Behavior: The Lease Disclosure Rule" Unpublished working paper (April 1986).

R. Leftwich. "Accounting Information in Private Markets: Evidence from Private Lending Agreements." *The Accounting Review* (January 1983), pp. 23–42.

R. Holthausen and R. Leftwich. "The Economic Consequences of Accounting Choice: Evidence from Private Lending Agreements." *Journal of Accounting and Economics*, 5 (August 1983), pp. 77–117.

C. Smith and J. Warner. "On Financial Contracting: An Analysis of Bond Covenants." *Journal of Financial Economics*, 7 (1982), pp. 117–161.

D. Thornton and M. Bryant. *GAAP (Generally Accepted Accounting Principles) vs. TAP (Tailored Accounting Principles) in Lending Agreements: Canadian Evidence* (The Canadian Academic Accounting Association, 1986).

R. Tighe. *Structuring Commercial Loan Agreements* (Warren, Gorham & Lamont, 1984).

Discussion of the Use of Off–Balance Sheet Financing to Circumvent Financial Covenant Restrictions

CLIFFORD W. SMITH, JR.*

El-Gazzar, Lilien, and Pastena (1988) examine forty-three private debt agreements negotiated prior to 1976 involving thirty different firms that were intensive lessees. They find that these contracts generally employ accounting-based constraints to restrict distributions to shareholders and to restrict additional debt issuance. The authors specifically note little tailoring of GAAP numbers to control off–balance sheet financing methods—specifically, the capitalization of lease obligations. The documented deviations from GAAP are generally quite simple—tailored accounting in financial contracts typically starts with GAAP and then eliminates noncash accruals.

I believe the authors should be commended for their work in this paper. They examine evidence that is not readily available, is difficult to acquire, and is ignored too often by the profession. If I have a problem with the paper, it is with balance. These are places where I believe there are potentially important considerations the authors do not discuss. Therefore, I will concentrate on these points in my discussion.

I believe the authors try too hard to motivate the paper in terms of a conflict between Abdel-khalik (1971), El-Gazzar, Lilien, and Pastena (1986), and Imhoff and Thomas (1986), who argue that the use of off–balance sheet items such as operating leases can reduce the constraints imposed on corporate policy choices through bond covenants, and Leftwich (1983) and Holthausen and Leftwich (1983), who argue that firms have incentives to specify covenants employing tailored accounting definitions (for example, the specification of lease capitalization). Rather than an ''academic conflict,'' I view this as simply two solutions to a common problem.

If a firm employs GAAP to specify constraints in bond covenants, then where GAAP permits discretion in the choice of techniques, firms have the latitude to choose the technique that makes the constraint least binding. Of course, both borrower and lender recognize this at contract origination. And since the lender has riskless lending opportunities, the costs of retaining this

*Professor, William E. Simon Graduate School of Business Administration, University of Rochester.

discretion are generally imposed on the borrower through higher promised interest payments.

If in the contract negotiation the borrower agrees to prespecify accounting practice and reduce its discretion in terms of how it reports the accounting values employed in the covenants, then lenders will generally accept lower promised interest payments. But this solution can impose other costs. If GAAP is changed over the life of the bond, such customized accounting numbers may become very expensive to produce. Thus, authors back to Smith and Warner (1979) have argued that the lower the cost of renegotiation, the more likely the firm will negotiate contracts employing tailored accounting numbers. Thus, Leftwich and Holthausen and Leftwich emphasize *ex ante* contracting incentives to control the problem, whereas Abdelkhalik, El-Gazzar et al., and Imhoff and Thomas focus on *ex post* implications of not employing tailored accounting numbers.

There are many ways that this trade-off between *ex ante* and *ex post* solutions to this problem could be addressed empirically. I think it is worth emphasizing that in this paper, the authors employ a nonrandom sample to examine the issue. This is important for an obvious reason: One should be careful in trying to generalize about the universe of debt contracts from a nonrandom sample of firms' bond covenants.

However, I think it is important for a less obvious reason as well. The authors focus on "intensive lessees" in selecting their sample. This helps ensure that the potential off–balance sheet leasing problem is significant. However, I believe that by itself it is insufficient to conclude that these firms are more likely to include specific provisions to control leasing. For example, one covenant sometimes observed in corporate indentures is a covenant against mergers. I would argue that if we were to examine indentures for a set of "intensive mergers," we would be unlikely to observe a single covenant against mergers—a merger covenant would impose too much disruption of such a firm's business.

I believe that to extract more from these data one needs to carefully examine each firm's incentives to lease. At times one gets the impression in this paper that the only reason to lease an asset is to keep the transaction off the balance sheet and thereby change the extent to which a covenant is binding. In Smith and Wakeman (1985), we argue that there are strong economic reasons to lease rather than buy various assets. It would be interesting to see if one could identify different economic motives for leasing across firms that employ the different covenants.

The profession is still struggling with developing an appropriate set of statistical tools to employ with data like these—it is hard to put a *t*-statistic on a dividend covenant. With respect to the data analysis, there is one final point where I would recommend caution. Although the authors examine forty-three contracts, they represent only thirty different borrower firms. I would suggest also examining the data employing the firm as the unit of observation. My experience with these contracts suggests there is more variability across firms than across contracts for a given firm. If so, then the second and third contracts for the same borrower are not independent observations.

In conclusion, I am encouraged to observe continuing empirical work producing a better understanding of the cross-sectional and time series variation in the use of these contracts. As this research accumulates, our understanding of these issues becomes steadily richer.

REFERENCES

Abdel-khalik, R. *Economic Effects on Leases of FASB Statement No. 13* (Stamford, Conn., 1971).

El-Gazzar, S., S. Lilien, and V. Pastena. "Accounting for Leases by Lessees." *Journal of Accounting and Economics* (1986), 217–237.

———. "The Use of Off–Balance Sheet Financing to Circumvent Financial Covenant Restrictions." Unpublished manuscript, 1988.

Holthausen, R., and R. Leftwich. "The Economic Consequences of Accounting Choice: Evidence from Private Lending Agreements." *Journal of Accounting and Economics* 5 (August 1983), pp. 77–117.

Imhoff, E., and S. Thomas. "Accounting Standards and Firm Behavior: The Lease Disclosure Rule." Unpublished working paper, April 1986.

Smith, Clifford, and L. Wakeman. "Determinants of Corporate Leasing Policy." *Journal of Finance* 40, no. 3 (July 1985), pp. 895–908.

Smith, Clifford, and J. Warner. "On Financial Contracting: An Analysis of Bond Covenants." *Journal of Financial Economics* 7 (1979), pp. 117–161.

Leftwich, R., "Accounting Information in Private Markets: Evidence from Private Lending Agreements," *The Accounting Review,* (January, 1983), pp. 23–42.

Debt Capacity and Financial Contracting: Finance Subsidiaries

JOSHUA RONEN* AND ASHWINPAUL C. SONDHI*

I. Introduction

In a recent Statement of Financial Accounting Standards (No. 94), the Financial Accounting Standards Board (FASB) amended Accounting Research Bulletin No. 51, *Consolidated Financial Statements,* to require consolidation of all majority-owned subsidiaries unless control is temporary or does not rest with the majority owner. Specifically, Statement 94 (October 1987) requires consolidation of a majority-owned subsidiary even if it has "nonhomogeneous" operations. The FASB viewed this Statement as "a major step in resolving the growing problem of off-balance sheet financing. Unconsolidated majority-owned subsidiaries have been a significant aspect of that problem. The growing size and importance of finance and other unconsolidated majority-owned subsidiaries and the resulting amounts of assets, liabilities, revenues, and expenses that have not been reflected in many consolidated financial statements have made the matter important" (para. 22).

One of the major concerns of the FASB, in particular, appears to have been the potential distortion of the debt-equity ratio caused by nonconsolidation of finance subsidiaries; "the paramount example is the debt-equity ratio, which, for reasons already described, is much lower if finance or other highly leveraged subsidiaries are accounted for by the equity method rather than consolidated. That effect is one aspect of off-balance-sheet financing that has been criticized because transactions between affiliates and intercompany receivables and payables often make it unlikely that 'do-it-yourself' consolidation can adequately approximate debt-equity ratios in consolidated financial statements provided by the enterprises themselves" (para. 40).

Some indirect justification for this concern is implied in the respondents' (to the Exposure Draft) offered reason for extending the effective date: "The risk of increased cost of borrowing at the time loan covenants are renegotiated would be mitigated if additional time was available" (para. 51).

The FASB's action to make overt off–balance sheet activities that hitherto have been partially covert (some of the activities have been indicated

*New York University.

in footnotes) raises some intriguing questions. Was the prior exemption from consolidation a motivating factor in creating finance subsidiaries with higher debt-equity ratios? Will Statement 94 induce management to decrease the level of debt? Would the parent companies creating the financial subsidiary have exhibited as high a debt-equity ratio had they not created such subsidiaries? If the ability of the managers not to consolidate had nothing to do with higher debt-equity ratios of the financial subsidiaries, is the requirement to consolidate justified?

The arguments presented in this paper, along with the evidence cited, yield tentative answers to some of these questions:

1. The incidence of high debt-equity ratios of consolidated entities that control a separate finance subsidiary is consistent with a theoretically motivated hypothesis that companies create finance subsidiaries in order to increase their debt capacity.
2. The creation of finance subsidiaries and the consequent increase in debt capacity change the risk-return posture of the company. Specifically, increase in debt capacity and in the actual debt-equity ratio— which increases returns to stockholders—is compensated for by additional risks imposed on stockholders (and possibly presubsidiary-creation debt holders).
3. The rationality of creating finance subsidiaries—increasing debt capacity and actual debt-equity ratios—is not related to accounting rules that either mandate consolidation or allow nonconsolidation. In other words, the accounting rule itself played no role in motivating creation of finance subsidiaries presumably to ''hide'' increased leverage.
4. Nonetheless, if the FASB argument quoted above, that do-it-yourself consolidation will not likely approximate debt-equity ratios in consolidated financial statements provided by the enterprises themselves is correct, then mandatory consolidation of finance subsidiaries seems to be justified.

The rest of the paper is organized as follows. Section II briefly documents the history of the creation of finance subsidiaries and the incidence of relatively high debt-equity ratios for companies that have created subsidiaries. Section III reviews studies that address the possible motivations of the creation of finance subsidiaries. A model derived in a companion paper (Sondhi, Fried, and Ronen [SFR, 1988]) is extended to develop the hypothesis that the creation of financial subsidiaries is consistent with the desire to increase debt capacity in Section IV. In Section V we provide an analysis of the covenants of financial subsidiaries that reflects the risks shifted to the stockholders to fa-

TABLE 1

A. Capital Funds* [$ in billions]

	1984	1985	1986	3-Year Growth Rate
Top 100 finance companies	$38.6(100)**	$44.4(100)	$52.1(100)	35%
Captives***	20.2(34)	22.5(36)	23.6(33)	17%
Independents/affiliates	18.4(66)	21.8(64)	28.5(67)	55%
Domestic bank-related firms	4.2(25)	5.3(26)	8.4(27)	100%

B. Subordinated Debt [$ in billions]

	1984	1985	1986	3-Year Growth Rate
Top 100 finance companies	$ 9.5(100)	$10.9(100)	$13.7(100)	40%
Captives	4.4(34)	4.2(36)	3.3(3.7)	−25%
Independents/affiliates	5.1(66)	6.7(64)	10.0(67)	96%
Domestic bank-related firms	1.3(25)	1.8(26)	2.9(27)	123%

C. Financial Ratios—19 Largest Finance Companies

	1984	1985	1986
Total debt/stockholders' equity	686%	759%	801%
Parent only: D/E	57%	59%	69%
Consolidated: D/E	332%	373%	332%

Source: The American Banker (June 13, 1986 and July 10, 1987), and Financial statements of firms used in Panel C.

*Capital funds include stockholders' equity and noncurrent subordinated debt.

**Numbers in parentheses reflect numbers of companies in the sample.

***Captives are subsidiaries whose operations are primarily dedicated to financing their parents' sales.

cilitate larger debt capacity. Concluding remarks and implications for future research are provided in the sixth and final section.

II. The Creation of Finance Subsidiaries and Their Leverage

The creation of finance subsidiaries has become an important business strategy of many nonfinancial companies. Capital funds of finance subsidiaries have grown by 35 percent during the past three years (see Table 1). The table compares the growth rate of finance subsidiaries with other finance companies that are not subsidiaries of financial corporations.

Wholly owned finance subsidiaries have been used to provide a wide array of financial services to their parents' customers and dealers. Some subsidiaries are captives in that at least 70 percent of their operations are dedicated to financing parent sales to customers and dealers. Other finance subsidiaries have developed into major financial intermediaries providing financial services beyond the requirements of their parents' manufacturing or retailing activities. They may finance the sales of other companies, engage in substantial leasing activities, and provide venture capital and leveraged buyout financing. Statement 94 does not make a distinction between finance subsidiaries that are captives and those that have become relatively independent from the standpoint of requiring consolidation. In our analysis presented below, we do not make any distinction either.

Along with the increase in finance subsidiaries, we observe a substantial increase in borrowing levels of the consolidated units that include finance subsidiaries relative to nonfinancial companies that have not created such subsidiaries. Panel C of Table 1 shows that some consolidated units that created finance subsidiaries have borrowed up to 3.7 times their equity compared with nonfinancial companies without subsidiaries, whose level of borrowing is no more than 58 percent of their equity.

This substantial leverage used by finance subsidiaries was kept off the parent companies' balance sheets, as a result of the ''nonhomogeneity'' of operations exemption allowed by financial reporting standards prior to Statement 94. Finance subsidiaries were included in their parents' financial statements under the equity method, whereby only the parent's share of the net assets and net income of the subsidiary was presented.

The coincidence of the creation of finance subsidiaries and the increase of leverage of the consolidated units within which they operate raises the question as to whether the ability to increase debt could have been one–if not the sole–motivation for the creation of finance subsidiaries. In the following section, the possible explanations for the creation of finance subsidiaries are examined through a brief review of the pertinent literature. This is followed by a brief description of SFR's model and further developments that demonstrate that, indeed, the expansion of debt capacity could be one of the motivations for the creation of finance subsidiaries.

III. Literature Review

Nonfinancial companies create finance subsidiaries by transferring cash flows embodied in financial assets (e.g., receivables in return for equity in the finance subsidiaries). The subsidiary finances these purchases by borrowing in the financial markets. The academic literature is divided with respect to the incentives for the creation of finance subsidiaries.

Hagaman (1969) suggested that the legal and financial segregation of finance subsidiaries may reduce the cost of monitoring and bonding activities since it facilitates the analysis of leverage and credit standing separately of the parent and the finance subsidiary. In a somewhat similar vein, Roberts and Viscione (1981) have viewed the creation of a finance subsidiary as a type of multidivisional reorganization effecting the separation of operating and strategic activities. This segregation would be accompanied, it is argued, by a more effective control system alleviating the task of monitoring by creditors and increasing borrowing capacity. In both of these cases no explanation is offered as to why legal separation is necessary to create a sufficiently effective internal control system for the other benefits to follow. In other words, the costs and benefits of the legal separation are not documented.

Andrews (1964) and Lewellen (1972) argue that the creation of the finance subsidiary results only in an illusory separation and does not increase debt capacity. Further, the observed leverage may actually increase the cost of capital to the total enterprise. Lewellen argues that the probability of default and debt obligations may increase and collateral values in liquidation may decline. Thus, the debt capacity of the total entity is either maintained at the same level or may decline. But this leaves us with no explanation for the popularity of creating finance subsidiaries.

The creation of finance subsidiaries is characterized as a capital structure rearrangement that violates a Me-First Rule by Kim, McConnell, and Greenwood (KMG, 1977). Me-First Rules are "prior arrangements that protect bondholders from uncompensated shifts of wealth to stockholders through a change in the capital structure of the firm" (KMG, p. 789). Thus, the creation of the finance subsidiary would result in a class of security holders with income claims superior to those of existing bondholders. The resulting windfall loss in wealth suffered by bondholders accrues to stockholders, since the analysis assumes that the spin-off will not increase the value of the firm. KMG further suggest that when a firm increases debt financing and simultaneously violates a Me-First Rule, stockholders will benefit additionally through the higher tax subsidy from increased debt that will increase the after-tax value of the firm. Left undiscussed by KMG is the possible increase in bankruptcy and agency costs brought upon by the high level of debt. But if KMG's contentions are correct, the puzzling questions would be why existing lenders to the nonfinancial corporation do not adequately protect themselves against the violation of the Me-First Rule in bond covenants. Surely, if they do protect themselves, then the alleged benefits claimed by KMG for the creation of subsidiaries—which are conditional on the violation of the Me-First Rule—would fail to materialize, and we are again left with no explanation as to why finance subsidiaries are created. Moreover, it is not clear who bears the increase, if any, in agency costs due to increased debt.

In the next section it is shown how with appropriate guarantees by the parent of the assets and profitability of the subsidiary, the debt capacity of the total entity can be increased. This increased debt capacity, which promises higher returns to stockholders, would be brought about by the willingness of stockholders to offer such guarantees as would impose additional risk on the stockholders and possibly the pre-subsidiary-creation bondholders. In other words, it will be contended that the creation of a finance subsidiary involves the movement of the entity into a new risk return posture–higher risk and higher return.

IV. A Model of Debt Capacity

SFR have shown under certain assumptions that the incorporation of a company as a parent and as a subsidiary can enable it to have a higher debt capacity than if it were to be incorporated as a single corporation. In this section we focus on the conditions under which a creation of a finance subsidiary can expand that capacity. We do this by developing a plausible scenario under which this capacity would be the same whether or not the company creates a finance subsidiary and contrast that with a scenario developed by SFR to focus on the conditions–in this case guarantees–that would make possible the expanded debt capacity. First we state below basic assumptions underlining both scenarios:

We consider a single firm in a one-period model where x represents its end-of-period cash flows including liquidation value of assets. The firm has a single bond issue outstanding and Y denotes the amount due at the end of the period. Thus, x represents the value of the firm, which equals the value of equity plus the value of debt. The value of equity is the value of a European option on x with the exercise price equaling Y. Hence the value of equity is:

$$E = \max [(x-Y), 0], \tag{1}$$

Whereas the value of debt is:

$$B = x-e = \min (Y, x), x > 0 \tag{2}$$

The assumption that $x > 0$ implies that losses of equity and bondholders are limited to the value of the assets. Conceivably, there could be negative cash flows (x less than 0) to the extent that liabilities are created that accrue to unsecured creditors such as employees and suppliers. Limiting x to be nonnegative would then imply that any such unsecured liabilities will be unsatisfied should x fall below the value of secured debt. It is also assumed that the remaining cash flows of the parent and the cash flows transferred to the subsidiaries are uncorrelated.

The value of the above debt obligation (D) is the present value of the debt value in equation (2) discounted at the risk-free interest rate, r:

$$D = (1 + r)^{-1} E [\min (Y, x)]$$

$$= (1 + r)^{-1} \int_0^\infty \min (Y, x) f (x) dx \qquad (3)$$

$$= (1 + r)^{-1} [Y - \int_0^Y F(x) dx] \text{ or } D (1 + r)$$

$$= Y - \int_0^Y F(x) dx.$$

This can be rewritten as:

$$i - r = \frac{1}{D} \int_0^Y F(x) dx = \frac{(1+i)}{Y} \int_0^Y F(x) dx \qquad (3a)$$

where

r   = risk-free interest rate, and
f(x) = density function of x.

In the situation described above, bondholders receive x when the cash flows of the firm lie between zero and x. They receive Y, the amount promised them, when realized cash flows equal or exceed Y.

And $Y/D = 1 + i$ to reflect the constraint that debt capacity, $D(i)$, must be evaluated at a given yield i. (Increased borrowing at higher yields does not reflect debt capacity increases.)

Equation (3a) has an appealing intuitive interpretation. $\int_0^Y F(x)dx$ can be interpreted as the expected total loss on the debt with total value D over the range of realizations that fall below the face amount of debt. Divided by D, we have the right hand side (r.h.s.), which constitutes the total expected percentage loss per dollar of debt, or average percentage loss. The equation merely states that this average percentage loss will be demanded as risk premium, $i - r$.

The conditions that might enable the company to expand debt capacity by creating a finance subsidiary is presented below through two scenarios.

In the first, bondholders of the subsidiary have prior claims to any cash realizations (x) up to the value of the financial assets (G) transferred to the subsidiary by the parent. This could realistically be the case either when the parent grants the subsidiary such priority (assuming the parent's bond covenants do not preclude this) or because by their very nature the financial assets transferred to the finance subsidiary are the least risky and, hence, the most likely to be converted into cash. Cash realizations beyond G (the financial assets transferred) would be by definition generated within the parent and will be earmarked for satisfying the debt of the parent up to the face value of that debt $y_{p'}$. The cash realizations above $Y_{p'} + G$ will then revert to the subsidiary for satisfying any of its additional outstanding debt up to the face value of that debt Y_s. (Although bondholders of the subsidiary may not be able to claim rights to these realizations, it is assumed that the parent would not let the subsidiary go bankrupt.) Any realizations beyond $G + Y_p + Y_s$ will accrue to stockholders.

The Appendix shows that, under these assumptions, the combined debt capacity of the parent (Y_{p1}) and the subsidiary (Y_{s1}) is given by:

$$(1 + r)D_1 = Y_1 - \int_0^{Y_1} F(x)dx, \tag{4}$$

where $D_1 = D_{p1} + D_{s1}$, D_{p1} = debt capacity of the parent, D_{s1} = debt capacity of the subsidiary, and $Y_1 = Y_{p1} + Y_{s1}$, and the numerical subscripts depict the scenario. Because equation (4) is identical to (3), we see that D_1 equals D, and Y_1 must equal Y (the two equations have identical solutions) and thus debt capacity is the same with or without a finance subsidiary in Scenario 1.

Note that, because of the priority accorded the subsidiary bondholders, there would be a wealth transfer to them from the parent's bondholders compared with the situation whereby only a single entity is involved, even though the total debt capacity is identical. This wealth transfer can be measured by $d_{w'}$, the difference between the value of subsidiary debt (see Appendix) and the subsidiary debtholders' proportional share of the value of total debt as follows:

$$d_w = Y_{s1} - \int_{Y_{p1}+G}^{Y_{p1}+Y_{s1}} F(x)dx - \int_0^G F(x)dx - \frac{Y_{s1}}{Y_{p1}+Y_{s1}}$$

$$[Y_{p1} + Y_{s1} - \int_0^{Y_{p1}+Y_{s1}} F(x)dx]$$

$$= \frac{Y_{p1}}{Y_1} \int_0^{Y_1} F(x)dx - \int_G^{Y_{p1}+G} F(x)dx$$

We now move to scenario 2. Here we assume that the financial assets transferred, G, either are riskless (such as cash or bank deposits) or are made virtually riskless to debtholders of the subsidiary by having the parent guaranteeing to the subsidiary the face value of the assets transferred (such as when the assets transferred are accounts receivable, and their book value is guaranteed by the parent). One way of implementing this guarantee, for example, would be by stockholders' contributing capital. The second scenario is analyzed by SFR, where it is shown that the combined debt capacity is:

$$(1 + r) D_2 = Y_2 - \int_0^{Y_2} F(x)dx + \int_0^G F(x)dx \tag{5}$$

or, in terms of premium:

$$(i - r) = \frac{1 + i}{Y_2} \int_0^{Y_2} F(x)dx - \frac{1 + i}{Y_2} \int_0^G F(x)dx. \tag{5a}$$

That the combined debt capacity is greater than that of Scenario 1 or, equivalently, greater than the capacity of a company without a subsidiary can be easily seen by comparing (5) with either (4) or, equivalently, (3). Because we insist on the same yield in both scenarios, we have from (3a) and (5a):

$$(i - r) = \frac{1 + i}{Y_2} \int_0^{Y_2} F(x)dx$$

$$(6)$$

$$- \frac{1 + i}{Y_2} \int_0^G F(x)dx = \frac{1 + i}{Y} \int_0^Y F(x)dx.$$

Denoting $(Y_2 - Y)$ by δ (difference in debt capacity evaluated at face value), (6) becomes:

$$\frac{1}{Y + \delta} \int_0^{Y+\delta} F(x)dx = \frac{1}{Y} \int_0^Y F(x)dx + \frac{1}{Y + \delta} \int_0^G F(x)dx. \quad (7)$$

Since the second r.h.s. term is positive, δ must be positive for the left hand side (l.h.s.) to be larger than the first r.h.s. term. Note that $F(y)$ is the marginal value of the function $\int_0^Y F(x)dx$ and the first r.h.s. term is the average; and because $F(x)$ is monotone increasing, the marginal exceeds the average and the average must increase in Y. That is:

$$\frac{\delta}{\delta Y} \left(\frac{1}{Y} \int_0^Y F(x)dx \right) = \frac{1}{Y} (F(Y)) - \frac{1}{Y} \int_0^Y F(x)dx > 0.$$

To establish lower and upper bounds for δ, the increase in debt capacity, rewrite (7) as:

$$\frac{1}{Y + \delta} \left(\int_0^Y F(x)dx + \int_y^{Y+\delta} F(x)dx - \int_0^G F(x)dx \right) = \frac{1}{Y} \int_0^Y F(x)dx$$

$$\int_0^Y F(x)dx + \int_0^{Y+\delta} F(x)dx - \int_0^G F(x)dx = \int_0^Y F(x)dx + \frac{\delta}{Y} \int_0^Y F(x)dx$$

$$\int_Y^{Y+\delta} F(x)dx - \frac{\delta}{Y} \int_0^Y F(x)dx = \int_0^G F(x)dx.$$

So:

$$F(Y)\delta - \frac{\delta}{Y} \int_0^Y F(x)dx \leq \int_0^G F(x)dx \leq F(Y+\delta)\delta - \frac{\delta}{Y} \int_0^Y F(x)dx.$$

From this we obtain:

$$\frac{\int_0^G F(x)dx}{F(Y+\delta) - \frac{1}{Y}\int_0^Y F(x)dx} \leq \delta \leq \frac{\int_0^G F(x)dx}{F(Y) - \frac{1}{Y}\int_0^Y F(x)dx} \tag{8}$$

It is immediately clear that for a given $F(x)$, δ increases in G, the financial assets transferred to the subsidiary, and decreases with the denominator. But note that the denominator is simply the excess of the marginal value of the function $\int_0^Y F(x)dx$ (evaluated at $Y + \delta$ for the lower bound and at Y for the upper bound) over its average value.

To gain further insight suppose we let $F(x)$ vary while maintaining $F(y)$, the value of the firm, $\int_0^\infty xf(x)dx$, and $\int_0^G F(x)dx$. Consider the difference between any two realizations of the upper-bound denominator corresponding to F_i and F_j such that:

$$F_i(y) - \frac{1}{Y}\int_0^Y F_i(x)dx > F_j(y) - \frac{1}{Y}\int_0^Y F_j(x)dx,$$

$$\text{where } F_i(y) = F_j(y) = F(y). \tag{9}$$

The upper bound of the increase in debt capacity is thus larger for F_j than it is for F_i by a magnitude that increases in:

$$[F_i(Y) - \frac{1}{Y}\int_0^Y F_i(x)dx] - [F_j(Y) - \frac{1}{Y}\int_0^Y F_j(x)dx]. \tag{10}$$

Thus, the larger the expression (10), the larger the increases in the upper bound of the increment in debt capacity made possible. To evaluate when

(10) becomes larger, multiply and divide by Y and add and subtract $\int_0^\infty xf(x)dx$ and $Y[1 - F(Y)]$ to obtain:

$$\frac{1}{Y} \{ (\int_0^\infty xf_i(x)dx - Y[1 - F_i(y)] - [YF_i(Y) - \int_0^Y F_i(x)dx])$$

$$- (\int_0^\infty x f_j(x)dx - Y[1 - F_j(Y)] - [YF_j(Y) - \int_0^Y F_j(x)dx]) \} \quad (11)$$

$$= \frac{1}{Y} \{ (\int_0^\infty xf_i(x)dx - \int_Y^\infty Yf_i(x)dx - \int_0^Y xf_i(x)dx$$

$$- (\int_0^\infty xf_j(x)dx - \int_Y^\infty Yf_j(x)dx - \int_0^Y xf_j(x)dx) \} \quad (12)$$

$$= \frac{1}{Y} [\int_Y^\infty (x - Y) f_i(x)dx - \int_Y^\infty (x - Y) f_j(x)dx]. \quad (13)$$

From (9), it is clear that the first term in the brackets is smaller than the second. The first is the value of equity under F_i and the second, the value of equity under F_j. Thus, changing F_i to F_j while keeping constant the values of $F(y)$, $\int_0^G F(x)dx)$, and $\int_0^\infty xf(x)dx$, increases δ, the increment of debt capacity made possible, by an amount directly proportional to the increase in the equity-debt ratio, a rather intuitively appealing observation.

Returning our attention to the numerator of (8) and allowing F to vary but fixing G, we see that the upper bound of δ increases with the probability that cash flows of the entity fall below G. That is, the larger the downside risk for the subsidiary's debt holders, the larger the value of the guarantee by stockholders of G and the larger the possible increase in debt capacity.

The lower bound of (8) yields similar interpretations and, hence, the above inferences apply to the behavior of δ in general vis-à-vis G, F, firm value, and initial debt; it also offers empirically testable implications conditional on data availability.

We now focus on the guarantee necessary to allow an increase in debt capacity. Comparing Scenarios 1 and 2, we find that unless G is made completely riskless, δ is zero, but a guarantee of G by the parent is worthless, as long as $\int_0^G F(x)dx$ is nonzero, or as long as there is any probability that total cash flows of the entity will fall below G. This means that the only way G can be guaranteed is by stockholders' committing to make personal capital contributions to supplement the cash flows of the entity up to G should they otherwise fall below it. This can clearly be seen by noticing that the value of the parents' debt is identical under Scenarios 1 and 2, but in Scenario 1 the cash flow of the parent alone is not allowed to fall below zero, whereas in Scenario 2 it can fall down to $-G$ so that the combined cash flows of the parent and the subsidiary do not fall below 0 while $+G$ is guaranteed to the subsidiary. This means that the equity holders can increase debt capacity by δ only if they *personally* guarantee cash flow deficiencies up to G. Thus, the undisclosed liability of the parent due to the off–balance sheet financing given rise to by subsidiary creation and the consequent enhancement in debt capacity could be quantified at:

$$\int_0^G (G - X)\, f(x)dx = G \int_0^G f(x) - \int_0^G xf(x)dx$$

$$= GF(G) - XF \Big|_0^G + \int_0^G F(x)dx$$

$$= \int_0^G F(x)dx. \tag{14}$$

Thus, $\int_0^G F(x)dx$ is the proper quantification of the equity holders' guarantee.

Note from (8) that it exceeds the increment in debt capacity by an amount that equals at least:

$$\int_0^G F(x)dx - \frac{\int_0^G F(x)dx}{F(y) - \frac{1}{Y}\int_0^Y F(x)dx} \geq \textit{actual} \text{ increase in debt capacity.}$$

Thus, even after consolidation under Statement 94, the value of equity holders' obligation *would not be fully reflected*.

In the next section we offer detailed examination of the debt covenants and operating agreement (between parent and subsidiary) by comparing pre-subsidiary-creation covenants with post-subsidiary-creation debt covenants. The purpose will be to ascertain whether the guarantees implied in the above analysis were indeed offered by equity holders to make possible the observed increase in debt capacity.

V. Data Collection

The various bond covenants and the operating agreements discussed below were derived from Moody's Industrial and Moody's Bank & Finance manuals. The data were augmented, where possible, by recourse to disclosures of loan agreements in the firms' annual reports and Form 10-K reports.

The covenants discussed below were obtained from loan agreements in publicly issued debt of forty companies. Twenty-two subsidiaries of manufacturing firms and seven finance subsidiaries of major retailing firms are included. Eleven financial services companies or their finance subsidiaries are also discussed in order to compare covenants observed in a different class of financial intermediary.

Debt covenants in loan agreements covering publicly issued debt of forty-four manufacturing and retailing companies are also discussed. These firms created finance subsidiaries during the 1964–1976 period. These firms were selected for two reasons: (1) We needed firms with seasoned finance subsidiaries with public debt outstanding, and (2) the parents were firms with public debt outstanding before and after the subsidiary was formed.

The availability of data is limited to a great extent by the fact that Moody's manuals provide data only on companies with public debt and the comprehensiveness of its coverage varies across firms. Another limitation is due to the fact that all firms do not disclose their loan agreements in the Form 10-K filings. Much of the data used in the operating agreements discussion is derived from periodic research reports developed by financial analysts.

Research on Bond Covenants

Smith and Warner (1979) provide a descriptive review of specific provisions of various covenants in debt contracts based on an American Bar Foundation publication, "Commentaries on Model Debenture Indenture Provisions 1965" (1971). "Commentaries" compiles the standardized provisions of loan agreements.

Smith and Warner document various dividend and financing policy constraints designed to control the conflict between bondholders and stockholders. Restrictions on production/investment policy were not observed, and it was hypothesized that these would be too costly and hence are not used.

Leftwich (1983) used a sample of private loan agreements of insurance companies in addition to "Commentaries." He found that accounting measurement rules in lending agreements differed systematically from generally accepted accounting principles (GAAP). The negotiated rules seemed to be designed to reduce the conflicts between bondholders and stockholders.

El-Gazzar, Lilien, and Pastena (1986) provide some conflicting evidence in the case of leases and suggest that managements' reporting choices are designed to mitigate the tightness of covenants in loan agreements. El-Gazzar, Lilien, and Pastena (1988) provide further evidence that management choices with respect to GAAP reporting of off–balance sheet financing activities allow them to circumvent some restrictions in loan agreements.

The review of covenants in finance subsidiary loan agreements and the operating agreement between the parent and subsidiary discussed below should augment our understanding of the role of covenants in controlling the bondholder-stockholder conflict. These covenants may also be compared with those documented by prior research.

The Operating Agreement

Operating agreements detail the rules governing transactions between the parent and its finance subsidiary. Generally, these agreements are observed between parent firms and their captive finance subsidiaries only. Operationally, a subsidiary conducting at least 70 percent of its operations with the parent is considered a captive. A few finance subsidiaries have expanded into various other types of financing operations, often providing financing for products of unrelated companies. The evaluation of changes, if any, in operating agreements as nonparent business becomes significant would be a useful extension of this research study.

The operating agreement serves as a critical link between the cash flows, financial assets, and borrowing activities since the captive derives a significant component of its economic substance from transactions with its parent. Various characteristics of the operating agreement are designed to reduce the risks inherent in cash flows derived from the parent's receivables purchased by the subsidiary. Other components seem designed to ensure liquidity and protection of collateral values for lenders. These different characteristics are discussed below in three categories:

A. The Income Maintenance Agreement
B. Holdback Reserves
C. Other

A. The Income Maintenance Agreement (IMA)

The IMA is probably the most important component, and it is observed in most operating agreements. Through the IMA, the parent guarantees that the subsidiary's net income will be a prespecified multiple of its fixed charges. The receivables (adjusted for uncollectibles) are sold at a discount, which allows the subsidiary's earnings to reach required multiples of finance charges. The operating agreements specify that receivables must be sold at discounts competitive with those prevailing in the financial markets. The parent makes direct payments to the subsidiary when its earnings are below required levels.

Table 2 details the significant characteristics of twenty operating agreements. Eleven firms have explicit IMAs guaranteeing that earnings will be 1.5 times their fixed charges. Section 81.2 of the New York Life Insurance Law designates debt securities of captives as legal reserve instruments when the captive has maintained this ratio for five years. One IMA guarantees coverage in terms of pretax income, and another allows interest payments to parent only if coverage is maintained at 1.5 times the external fixed charges.

Three retail finance subsidiaries and one manufacturing subsidiary have no explicit IMAs. However, the parent firms have agreed to maintain subsidiary earnings. Insurance companies purchase their debt securities on the basis of credit experience and these "moral" maintenance agreements. Finally, two firms have no IMAs. One does not have an explicit IMA, but maintenance of coverage is required by loan agreements.

B. Holdback Reserves

The operating agreement often allows the subsidiary to withhold a predetermined portion of the purchase price to be refunded when the receivables are collected. The portion of the purchase price withheld is called the holdback reserve.

Table 2 shows that eight companies have no explicit holdback reserves. These firms have receivables with high collateral values, and the underlying products are easier to repossess and resell. The six retail finance subsidiaries contain holdback provisions since they purchase receivables with low collateral values.

C. Other

Operating agreements often allow the subsidiary the right to select receivables and employ its own credit analysis. The agreements detail the

TABLE 2

Characteristics of Operating Agreements

	Type of Subsidiary (Number of firms)	
	Subsidiaries of Manufacturing Firms (14)	Subsidiaries of Retailers (6)
1. Income Maintenance Agreements:		
a. Explicit	8	3
b. Moral	1	3
c. Other	3	
d. None	2	
2. Holdback Reserve		
a. Explicit	6	6
b. None	8	
3. Repurchase Agreement with Parent		
a. Explicit	9	2
b. Limited	2	—
c. None	3	4
4. Joint Bank Credit Lines		
a. Explicit	6	3
b. None	8	3
5. Termination Rights		
a. Explicit	10	5
b. Limited	3	—
c. None	1	1

Notes

Income Maintenance Agreement (IMA)

Generally, the IMA requires the parent to guarantee the subsidiary's earnings at 1.5 times the fixed charges. Companies with moral (M) IMA don't have explicit statements in the operating agreement, but their practice has implied these conditions.

Holdback Reserve

The holdback or dealer reserves range from 5 to 10 percent of receivables outstanding.

Repurchase Agreement

The repurchase agreement specifies the price and conditions under which the parent will refund or repurchase defaulted contracts. The limited agreement specifies particular types of defaulted receivables that the parent will purchase.

Termination Rights

Generally, either company has the right to terminate the agreement with some notice. Rights may be limited by provision of debt agreements. Termination rights are of limited duration, and may require consent of lenders of senior and subordinated debt.

parent's responsibilities in the event of default and the assistance it will provide through repossession and the payments it must make to the subsidiary on repossession.

The majority of agreements allow either the parent or the subsidiary to terminate agreements with a short notice period. One company requires lender consent and another requires redemption of public debt before termination. The agreements also provide for joint bank credit lines ensuring subsidiary access to credit markets.

VI. Analysis of the Operating Agreement

The parent-subsidiary structure contributes to the development of a more effective internal control system through contractual provisions that allow the subsidiary to use its own credit analyses to select receivables for purchase. The operational and legal segregation from the parent may increase the probability of rejecting poor-credit-quality receivables.

The liquidity and collateral values of receivables are enhanced by provisions detailing the parent's responsibilities in the events of default and repossession. Thus, the parent bears the cost of poor-credit-quality receivables, defaults, and repossessions.

The subsidiary's investment in the selected receivables (its purchase price) is the discounted present value of the receivables' expected cash flows (i.e., net of uncollectibles). The costs of uncollectibles are borne by the parent, reducing the risks of the subsidiary's cash flows.

The holdback reserve constitutes additional parent equity investment in the subsidiary and additional guarantee of the subsidiary's cash flows. The covenants requiring minimum levels of investment in receivables ensure continued sales by the parent, which preserves a minimum holdback reserve or parent equity in the subsidiary (see the discussion on Refunding and Call Provisions).

The IMAs guarantee minimum coverage of the subsidiary's fixed charges. Thus, the receivables must be discounted at a rate allowing the achievement of this minimum coverage, but the discount rate must be competitive with prevailing market rates. When the subsidiary's earnings are below required levels, the parent makes direct subsidy payments to make up the shortfall.

The IMA guarantees the cash flows of the subsidiary at some multiple of its fixed costs and the parent bears this cost directly through required subsidies. The IMA also provides incentives to manage the subsidiary's borrowing to minimize the drains on the parent's cash flows. The required minimum coverage ratio may be stated as:

$$\text{Subsidiary's Return on Equity} > d \times \frac{D}{E} (K-1)$$

where

d = pretax cost of debt,

$\dfrac{D}{E}$ = leverage ratio, and

K = required coverage ratio.

Source: Unpublished research report prepared by an Investment Bank

The above formulation shows that for a given level of required coverage, the subsidiary's required return on equity increases as its pretax cost of debt and degree of leverage increases. The parent can control or manage required cash transfers to the subsidiary through a controlled growth of leverage and subsidiary interest costs or by additional infusions of equity funds in the subsidiary.

Thus, the IMA acts in concert with restrictions on additional debt, dividend restrictions, and minimum levels of receivables, all of which specify minimum levels of parent equity investment in the subsidiary. Excessive leverage or borrowing at higher cost triggers subsidy payments and/or additional equity investment by the parent.

Dividend Restrictions

Table 3 depicts two types of dividend restrictions in the sample firms. Fourteen firms have covenants limiting dividends below specified consolidated net income and proceeds from sale of stock after issue date. Eighteen firms have covenants disallowing dividends unless consolidated current assets are some specified percentage of consolidated current liabilities, all funded and current debt, or some combination thereof. Eight firms did not have dividend restrictions.

All the financial services firms exhibit dividend restrictions. Finance subsidiaries of all retailing firms exhibit more restrictive covenants. The largest finance subsidiaries have no dividend restrictions (e.g., General Motors Acceptance Corp. and General Electric Credit Corp.).

The theoretical model developed in Section IV suggests that the parent-subsidiary structure allows an increase in debt capacity that is driven by the negotiation of guarantees of subsidiary assets and profitability. The observed dividend restrictions support this contention by constraining the parent's ability to reduce subsidiary liquidity or dilute the value of bondholders' claims by paying dividends from proceeds of new debt issues. The restric-

TABLE 3

Dividend Restrictions

BASIS

Type of Subsidiary (Number of Firms)		Cumulative Profitability Plus Equity Proceeds (A)	Excess of Net Worth or Current Assets over Debt (B)	None
1. Subsidiaries of manufacturing firms	(22)	9	7	6
2. Subsidiaries of retailers	(7)	—	5	2
3. Subsidiaries of financial services firms or independents	(11)	5	6	—
Total	40	14 (35%)	18 (45%)	8 (20%)

Notes:

(A) Company may not pay cash dividends on or acquire capital stocks in excess of (i) consolidated net income of company and (ii) proceeds from sale of stock after specified date (generally, the report date immediately preceding the issue date).

(B) Company may not declare or pay any dividends or make any distribution (except in common stock) on or retire (except by exchange of stock, conversion of preferred into common, or redemption of preferred through new issues) any stock, directly or indirectly, unless immediately thereafter consolidated current assets (as defined) equal at least 120 percent of the sum of (i) all consolidated funded and current debt (as defined), (ii) par or involuntary liquidation value of unowned outstanding stock of restricted subsidiaries ranking prior to their common, and (iii) minority stock interests of restricted subsidiaries at net worth.

tions on reacquisition of equity also limit the parent's ability to effect a reduction in its equity investment in the subsidiary.

These covenants reinforce the minimum, continuing investment required by the provisions for holdback reserves which would be meaningless if the parent could drain subsidiary cash flows through dividends or reduce their equity investment through stock reacquisitions.

Kalay (1979) argues that the maximum restriction on dividends essentially implies a requirement for minimum investment by equity holders. Note that when a firm creates a finance subsidiary, it generally holds all the equity in the subsidiary; thus, the existence of dividend and stock reacquisition constraints implies the parent's willingness to meet minimum equity investment standards.

Smith and Warner suggest that the dividend constraint reduces the underinvestment problem discussed in Myers (1977) since the firm will reject fewer profitable projects if it must maintain equity investment of some minimum amount. Thus, the dividend constraint serves as a proxy for restrictions on production/investment policy.

The observed dividend constraints are based on cumulative profitability or various measures of net worth of the subsidiary, implying continued, minimum investment by the parent. The restrictions based on net worth have the added characteristic of constraining revenue and expense recognition methods used by management since income recognition directly affects reported levels of receivables that account for a majority of the assets reported by finance companies, thereby requiring continued minimum investment by the parent.

The FASB issued a new revenue and expense recognition standard (FASB, 1986) that limits the available recognition methods. The relationship between dividend restrictions and recognition methods may provide further insights into the contracting process.

Limitations on Additional Debt

Table 4 shows restrictions on additional debt ranging from restrictions on senior debt to limitations on junior subordinated debt. They either are expressed in maximum dollar amounts or require the maintenance of various ratios. Senior debt is limited to some multiple of the capital base; some aggregate of senior, junior, and parent subordinated debt; and liquid net worth or some multiple of net worth. Similar restrictions on subordinated debt were observed.

A few firms have covenants requiring net receivables to be some multiple of various classes of debt or net worth. Others have restrictions on amounts invested in nonfinance subsidiaries (an investment restriction) and a requirement for a minimum stockholders' equity. Finally, some restrictions on various classes of off–balance sheet financing are observed.

The observed limitations on additional debt seem designed to limit senior debt to some prespecified multiple of the underlying capital base, which is defined to include parent equity in the subsidiary and subordinated debt including subordinated debt owed to the parent. The subordinated debt limitations are often defined in terms of parent equity plus earnings retained in the subsidiary.

Thus, the allowed debt (senior and subordinated) generally is restricted to a prespecified multiple of the parent's direct equity investment or may include some subordinated debt owed to the parent. These restrictions effectively guarantee specific levels of parent equity investment in the subsidiary.

The provisions limiting additional debt to a specific multiple of the capital base limit dividend payments or reduce the ability of the firm to finance dividend payments through debt issuance.

Finally, some firms exhibit restrictions on investment in nonfinance

TABLE 4

Additional Debt Restrictions

Type of Subsidiary (Number of firms)		On Senior Debt (Type of Restrictions)		On Subordinated Debt (Type of Restriction)		Other	
1. Subsidiaries of manufacturing firms	(22)	A B C D None	6 1 1 0 14	A B C D None	4 7 9 1 3	A B C	2 1 1
2. Subsidiaries of retailers	(7)	A B C D None	— — — — 7	A B C D None	— — 4 1 2	A B C	1 — —
3. Subsidiaries of financial services firms of independents	(11)	A B C D None	1 — — 1 10	A B C D None	— — 8 — 3	A B C	— — —

Notes on Additional Debt Restrictions
On Senior Debt:

   (A) Senior debt may not exceed 400 percent (500 percent) of capital base.*

   (B) Senior debt may not exceed 4 times adjusted capital base. Senior debt must include subordinated debt in excess of 40 percent (50 percent) of capital base.

   (C) Senior debt may not exceed 375 percent of the sum of total senior, junior, and parent subordinated debt plus liquid net worth.

   (D) Aggregate outstanding debt of company and subsidiaries may not exceed 925 percent of consolidated adjusted net worth.

   *Capital base = Equity + subordinated debt (including subordinated debt owed parent)
On Subordinated Debt:

   Company or restricted subsidiary may not incur any debt other than

   (A) Subordinated debt of company up to 50 percent of capital base less subordinated debt.

   (B) Junior subordinated debt of company up to 50 percent of capital base less subordinated debt plus junior subordinated debt.

   (C) Subordinated debt up to 125 percent of consolidated capital stock, surplus, and capital debt. Any subordinated or junior subordinated debt up to 150 percent of consolidated capital stock, surplus, and capital debt.

   (D) Senior subordinated debt up to junior subordinated debt plus liquid net worth *or* may be defined in terms of senior or junior subordinated debt up to 125 percent of parent subordinated debt plus liquid net worth.
Other:

   (A) Eligible net receivables, cash, and other investments must be at least 100 percent of total liabilities *or* at least 120 percent of the excess of senior debt over the sum of cash and the market value of direct U.S. government obligations, or ineligible receivables must be less than 5 percent of total assets.

   (B) Capital base less investment in nonfinance unconsolidated subsidiaries must exceed specified limits.

   (C) Stockholders equity must exceed specified amount.

TABLE 5

Call Provisions

Type of Subsidiary (Number of firms)		Call Provisions	None
1. Subsidiaries of manufacturing firms	(22)	14	8
2. Subsidiaries of retailers	(7)	5	2
3. Subsidiaries of financial services firms or independents	(11)	8	3
Total	40	27	13

The provisions normally specify calls at premium or par as a function of the total amount of receivables at a point in the time preceding redemption notice; many agreements prohibit calls through refunding at interest cost lower than coupon of said debt issue.

subsidiaries or constrain receivables to some multiple of debt or net worth. These covenants limit the parent's ability to engage in asset substitution or invest in projects that would dilute bondholder claims. The requirement for maintaining receivable levels reinforces the equity investment implied in the holdback reserve and preserve the collateral available in the subsidiary.

The restrictions on off-balance sheet financing are in accord with Smith and Warner's suggestion that these limitations alleviate underinvestment problems discussed in Myers and prevent claim dilution by limiting the ability to create senior claims through leasing.

Refunding and Call Provisions

Table 5 shows that twenty-seven of forty firms in the sample contain call provisions specifying premiums to be paid when bonds are refunded under declining business conditions. Generally, if receivables are between 60 and 80 percent of a specified maximum level attained previously, out-standing debt may be redeemed at specified premiums. Further, they stipulate that debt cannot be redeemed if refunding with lower coupon debt is planned. Redemption of short-term debt is required if senior debt is redeemed. These covenants are designed to preserve collateral values and may reduce the variance of the capital value of debt.

The requirement for premiums also acts as a deterrent to investment in nonfinancial assets, which is often restricted through separate covenants. The call provision acts in concert with the dividend restrictions to ensure protection to lenders. If the equity investment declines below a specified level or overall investment declines, the bondholders are protected further by these call provisions. Since debt cannot be redeemed if refunding is

TABLE 6

Bond Restrictions of the Parent Firms

	No. of Firms (Percentage of Total)	
Restriction	Preformation	Postformation
1. Dividends	36 (82%)	32 (80%)
2. Limitations on additional debt	28 (64%)	24 (60%)
3. Minimum current ratio or working capital or net assets requirement	18 (41%)	16 (40%)
4. Sale-leaseback limitations	14 (31%)	17 (43%)
Total firms in sample	44	40

contemplated at a lower coupon, the lenders to the subsidiary have significant protection against subsequent declines in interest rates. Thus, the premium requirements under declining business conditions and the limitations on redemption through refunding significantly reduce volatility of subsidiary debt.

Thirteen of the forty firms in the sample do not have call provisions under declining receivable conditions. Further research may provide insights into the underlying reasons. Firm size or financial leverage levels do not appear to be relevant factors. Call provisions are also observed in eight of the eleven financial services firms, which suggests they are not limited to finance subsidiaries of nonfinancial parents but are typical of various types of financial intermediaries.

Financial Contracting in the Parent

This section compares bond covenants in parent company loan agreements to those observed in financial subsidiary loan agreements to develop further insights into the financial contracting process and the debt capacity argument presented in Section IV.

It also reports a comparison of bond covenants in pre- and postformation loan agreements of companies forming finance subsidiaries. Our objective is to provide insights into issues raised by KMG; that is, do companies violate Me-First Rules when they create finance subsidiaries? Related issues involve restrictions, if any, on the creation of finance subsidiaries and whether agreements need to be renegotiated when finance subsidiaries are created.

A. Parent versus Subsidiary Loan Agreements

Direct restrictions on production/investment policy are not observed in parent company agreements. Smith and Warner have suggested that this may be due to excessive monitoring and legal costs that may result from probable bondholder control when production/investment policy is restricted.

However, Zinbarg (1975) argues that private-placement agreements may restrict the parents' investment in the subsidiary, which would serve to regulate cash flows from the parent to the subsidiary providing additional protection to the parent's bondholders. These restrictions may also exclude parent investment in the subsidiary from net worth calculations, thereby reinforcing the investment limitations through restrictive financial policy covenants defined in terms of net worth.

Covenants in finance subsidiary loan agreements limit their investments to various categories of financial assets. Provisions in operating agreements that allow for market-based tests of discount rates used to compute the purchase price of a substantial portion of these financial assets further strengthen these investment policy limitations. Smith and Warner suggested that it would be costly, if not impossible, to monitor management decisions to reject certain projects. The monitoring problem may be reduced or nullified for finance subsidiaries since lenders to the subsidiary are protected in the event of declining business conditions through various call provisions discussed above. Parent loan agreements exhibit minimum working capital and net worth requirements which work as warning signals protecting against declining investment (see American Bar Foundation [1971]).

Dividend and financing policy covenants are observed in both types of firms and appear to be stricter for finance subsidiaries. It is likely that their higher financial leverage is possible due to the tighter restrictive covenants which specify debt limitations as functions of minimum equity investments. The minimum equity requirement is strengthened by requirements for holdback reserves and other provisions of the operating agreement.

B. Pre- versus Postformation Loan Agreements

Table 6 provides a summary of bond covenants found in pre- and postformation public loan agreements of forty-four parent companies that formed finance subsidiaries during the 1964-1976 period.

A comparison of loan agreements of these companies shows no significant differences between dividend, debt, and other covenants before and after the formation of the subsidiaries. Fewer dividend restrictions were observed in the postformation loan agreements since that sample contains four fewer loan agreements. The only discernible increase occurs with respect to limitations on sale-leaseback arrangements. Given the lack of change in other restrictions, it is difficult to relate this increase to the formation of the subsidiary.

No evidence was found to suggest restrictions on the creation of finance subsidiaries in the preformation loan agreements. Similarly, we found no indications of renegotiations of loan agreements on formation.

From this evidence gathered on pre- and postformation debt covenants of the parent, the evaluation of operating agreements, and the comparison of debt covenants across different types of finance subsidiaries, it seems that the conditions stipulated for Scenario 1 have clearly been met; that is, the parents effectively guarantee the profitability and the book value of the financial assets transferred to their subsidiaries. However, we could not find direct evidence that indicated that a commitment by the parent's stockholders to guarantee the book value of transferred financial assets were cash flows generated by the entity to fall below the book value of the assets transferred. Nonetheless, as Gorton and Pennacchi (1988) suggest, it is plausible that reputation effects induce bondholders of the subsidiary to perceive precisely such implicit commitments on the part of the parent's stockholders to contribute capital in the event of adverse cash flow conditions. This may be sufficient to accord realism to Scenario 2.

VII. Conclusions

This paper constitutes the first step in a comprehensive evaluation of bond covenants found in the loan agreements of finance subsidiaries. It detailed the operating agreements between the parents and their captive finance subsidiaries. Many operating agreements include income maintenance agreements whereby the parent guarantees the profitability and the cash flows of the subsidiary. The holdback reserve provides additional parent equity in the subsidiary. Joint credit lines, repurchase agreements, and guarantees of continued sales of receivables were also observed.

The subsidiary loan agreements include dividend, financing policy, and investment policy restrictions. These limitations seem designed to protect the lenders and their investment in the subsidiary. A covenant defining premiums to be paid when debt is redeemed under declining business conditions is also observed. Various additional debt restrictions specifying levels of different classes of debt and their interrelationship are observed and discussed. The high degree of financial leverage used by finance subsidiaries may be facilitated by these extensive covenants defining the business relationship between the parent and the subsidiary, and the stringent limits on dividend, financing, and investment policy.

Finally, a brief discussion of the differences between parent and subsidiary covenants is provided. The impact of subsidiaries on existing agreements and the analysis of differences between public and private loan agreements is left to future research.

We found no evidence that stockholders committed to contribute capital sufficient to guarantee the value of assets transferred to the subsidiary. This implies that, given the parent's reputation and financial position, either subsidiary debt holders perceived the assets supporting their claim as riskless or they perceived parent guarantees as including stockholders' voluntary commitment to contribute capital. The less appealing explanation is irrationality.

APPENDIX

Parent debt $=$

$$(1+r)D_{pl} = \int_{G}^{Y_{pl}+G} (x-G)f(x)dx + \int_{Y_{pl}+G}^{\infty} Y_{pl}f(x)dx$$

$$= Y_{pl} - \int_{G}^{Y_{pl}+G} F(x)dx$$

Subsidiary debt $=$

$$(1+r)D_{sl} = \int_{0}^{G} xf(x)dx + G \int_{G}^{Y_{pl}+G} f(x)dx$$

$$+ \int_{Y_{pl}+G}^{Y_{pl}+Y_{sl}} (x - Y_{pl})f(x)dx + Y_{sl} \int_{Y_{pl}+Y_{sl}}^{\infty} f(x)dx = GF(G)$$

$$- \int_{0}^{G} F(x)dx + GF(Y_{pl} + G) - GF(G) + xF(x) \Big|_{Y_{pl}+G}^{Y_{p}+Y_{sl}}$$

$$- \int_{Y_{pl}+G}^{Y_{pl}+Y_{sl}} F(x)dx - Y_{pl}[F(Y_{pl} + Y_{sl}) - F(Y_{pl}+G)] + Y_{sl}[1-F(Y_{pl}+Y_{sl})]$$

$$= - \int_{0}^{G} F(x)dx + GF(Y_{pl} + G) + (Y_{pl}+Y_{sl})F(Y_{pl}+Y_{sl})$$

$$- (Y_{pl}+G)F(Y_{pl}+G)$$

$$- \int_{Y_{pl}+G}^{Y_{pl}+Y_{sl}} F(x)dx - Y_{pl}F(Y_{pl} + Y_{sl}) + Y_{pl}F(Y_{pl} + G)$$

$$+ Y_{sl}[1 - F(Y_{pl} + Y_{sl})] = Y_{sl} - \int_{Y_{pl}+G}^{Y_{pl}+Y_{sl}} F(x)dx - \int_{0}^{G} F(x)dx$$

Total debt $=$

$$Y_{pl} + Y_{sl} - \int_{G}^{Y_{pl}+G} F(x)dx - \int_{Y_{pl}+G}^{Y_{pl}+Y_{sl}} F(x)dx - \int_{0}^{G} F(x)dx =$$

$$= Y_{pl}+Y_{sl} - \int_{G}^{Y_{pl}+Y_{sl}} F(x)dx - \int_{0}^{G} F(x)dx = Y_{pl}+Y_{sl} - \int_{0}^{Y_{pl}+Y_{sl}} F(x)dx$$

REFERENCES

American Bar Foundation. "Commentaries on Model Debenture Indenture Provisions 1965" (1971).

American Institute of Certified Public Accountants. Accounting Research Bulletin No. 51, *Consolidated Financial Statements* (New York: AICPA, 1959).

Andrews, V .L. "Captive Finance Companies." *Harvard Business Review* (July–August 1964), pp. 80–92.

Captive Finance Companies, Privately circulated research report, 1978.

El-Gazzar, S., S. Lilien, and V. Pastena. "Accounting for Leases by Lessees." *Journal of Accounting and Economics* (October 1986), pp. 217–237.

El-Gazzar, S., S. Lilien, and V. Pastena. "Does Off–Balance Sheet Financing Allow Firms to Circumvent Financial Covenant Restrictions?" (Unpublished paper, Baruch College of CUNY, March 1988).

Financial Accounting Standards Board. Statement No. 91, *Accounting for Nonrefundable Fees and Costs Associated with Originating or Acquiring Loans and Initial Direct Costs of Leases* (Stamford, Conn.: FASB, 1986).

Financial Accounting Standards Board. Statement No. 94, *Consolidation of All Majority-Owned Subsidiaries* (Stamford, Conn.: (FASB, 1987).

Gorton, G. and G. Pennacchi, "Are Loan-Sales Really Off-Balance Sheet?" See chapter in this volume.

Hagaman, T. C. "Significance of a Captive Finance Subsidiary." *Commercial and Financial Chronicle* (October 23, 1969), pp. 1284–1286.

Kalay, A. "Towards a Theory of Corporate Dividend Policy." (Unpublished Ph.D. thesis, University of Rochester, 1979).

Kim, E. H., J.J. McConnell, and P. R. Greenwood. "Capital Structure Rearrangements and Me-First Rules in an Efficient Market." *Journal of Finance* (June 1977), pp. 789–810.

Leftwich, R. "Accounting Information in Private Markets: Evidence from Private Lending Agreements." *The Accounting Review* (January 1983), pp. 23–42.

Lewellen, W. "Finance Subsidiaries and Corporate Borrowing Capacity." *Financial Management* (Spring 1972), pp. 21–31.

Myers, S., "Determinants of Corporate Borrowing." *Journal of Financial Economics*, 5, (1977), pp. 147–175.

Reiser, C. "The Great Credit Pump." *Fortune* (February 1963), pp. 122–124, 148–157.

Roberts, G. and J. Viscione. "Captive Finance Subsidiaries and the M-Form Hypothesis." *The Bell Journal of Economics* 12, no. 1 (Spring 1981), pp. 285–295.

Smith, C. and J. Warner, "On Financial Contracting: An Analysis of Bond Covenants." *Journal of Financial Economics*, 7, (1979), pp. 117–161.

Sondhi, A. C., D. Fried, and J. Ronen. "Finance Subsidiaries and Debt Capacity" (Unpublished paper, New York University, 1988).

Zinbarg, E. D. "The Private Placement Loan Agreement." *Financial Analysts Journal* (July–August 1975), pp. 33–35, 52.

Discussion of Debt Capacity and Financial Contracting: Finance Subsidiaries

Jacob G. Birnberg*

Ronen and Sondhi's paper (1988) has a bit of the flavor of a good "whodunit" in both its research question and the manner in which it reaches its conclusion. Since the staging of "whodunits" is presently a very popular diversion, it may be interesting to take up their theme and review the paper with it in mind. In the case of both the paper at hand and a mystery, we observe the same three questions. These are:

- The nature of the crime and the victim.
- The perpetrator.
- The intent or motivation of the perpetrator.

Thus the role of the discussant is easily characterized. My objective is to review the evidence Ronen and Sondhi offer and consider how well it fits with other available evidence and the additional analysis they have offered.

The Research Issue

Ronen and Sondhi focus on the question of the existence of captive finance companies (CFCs) and the effect their nonconsolidation has on the various parties. However, rather than start with the assumption that the CFCs are an attempt to confuse the users as many critics of financial disclosure might have done, they begin with the notion that CFCs have an economic reason for existing. If they are correct, there may be no crime, no victim, and, of course, no perpetrator. The seemingly suspicious state of affairs that has been observed would then be explainable.

To ascertain the answer to the question of whether there is a legitimate economic purpose for the CFCs, Ronen and Sondhi tell a reasonable story. They argue that vertical integration into the finance area has benefits to the firm. These benefits will accrue to the parent firm's shareholders without harming the debt holders of the CFC.

Others have asserted this before (Hagaman [1969]). However, Ronen and Sondhi offer support for their position both analytically and with limited empirical data. Analytically they attempt to show that the benefits to the

---

*Professor of Business Administration, Katz Graduate School of Business, University of Pittsburgh.

parent firm's shareholders should accrue. With this formulation I have only two questions:

- How does the assumption (p. 10) that the cash flows from the assets sold to the CFC and the cash flows remaining with the parent are uncorrelated affect the analysis?
- What role might the incentives of the parent firm's managers play in the analysis?

It is easy to imagine in a CFC cases where the flows could be correlated to a reasonable degree. I have no idea of how that affects Ronen and Sondhi's analysis of the problem. However, if it proves to be critical, the results may be less general than they argue, and other possible explanations may still be reasonable.

The model presented in this paper does not explicitly consider the role of managerial incentives. Admittedly, there is a limit on what the authors can be expected to consider in any single paper. In the formulation offered here, managers are viewed as behaving as if their interests are the same as those of the shareholders of the parent company. Perhaps through stock purchase, stock options, or some other stock price–based incentive scheme, the income or wealth of the managers is contingent on the behavior of stock price. This is the same consideration that would motivate the parent firm's shareholders. In such a situation the concerned parties would appear to reduce from two, shareholders and managers, effectively to only one. That single group would include *both* the shareholders *and* the managers.

If the manager's compensation is closely related to the parent company's income and equity accounting and consolidation accounting offer divergent measures of the parent firm's profit, then incentives are an issue that cannot be ignored. The incentive effects would provide the motive for the crime, and the victims at the very least would be the shareholders of the parent firm.

The Empirical Evidence

Ronen and Sondhi include a significant amount of empirical evidence which reflects two important points:

- There are data consistent with Ronen and Sondhi's analytical work.
- The evidence is limited and not easily obtained.

Both of these are important. The presence of confirmitory evidence in the data would suggest (to continue the mystery theme) that not all of our potential suspects are guilty. (Indeed, this is *not* derivative of Agatha Christie's *Murder on the Orient Express*.) However, as Ronen and Sondhi indicate

(p. 20), the evidence is not easily obtained. Firms are not forthcoming with all the information in all cases. In a similar vein, we all are aware that some firms already consolidate their financial subsidiaries, whereas others do not. Thus, there may be reason to believe that all the firms are not the same. There may be firms that behave as Ronen and Sondhi conclude from their analysis. However, there may be other firms whose managements are interested in benefiting themselves or the parent firm's shareholders at the expense of the debt holders of the parent and, perhaps, the debt holders of the CFC as well.

If it is true that the firms establishing CFCs are a mixed bag of the "innocent" and the "guilty," the issue becomes one of modeling two situations, not merely one as Ronen and Sondhi do. What permits some of the firms to behave as they do, and why is management able to do so? Given the recent change in GAAP, we soon will have a data base reflecting the impact of FASB Statement 94. These data may answer some of the questions raised by Ronen and Sondhi's work as well as those raised by others at this conference.

Conclusion

Overall, I still am not sure whether the phenomenon of CFCs is a legitimate business practice intended to benefit the shareholders of the parent without harming the debt holders of the CFC or whether it reflects an attempt to take advantage of an accounting loophole to hide the true nature of the debt-equity ratio. The situation offered by CFCs is too tempting for me to believe that it reflects solely good intentions, as Ronen and Sondhi's model suggests. Fortunately, we probably will not have to wait too long to find out where the truth is. What *that* answer will be, I cannot say. However, I am confident that the subsequent empirical work in this area will benefit from Ronen and Sondhi's extensive and stimulating analysis of this interesting problem.

REFERENCES

Financial Accounting Standards Board. Statement No. 94, *Consolidation of All Majority-Owned Subsidiaries* (Stamford, Conn.: FASB, 1987).

Hagaman, T. C. "Significance of a Captive Finance Subsidiary." *Commercial and Financial Chronicle* (October 23, 1969), pp. 1284–1286.

Ronen, J., and A. C. Sondhi. "Debt Capacity and Financial Contracting: Finance Subsidiaries." Paper presented at the N.Y.U. Conference on Off–Balance Sheet Activities, May 13, 1988.

Appendix

TABLE 1

Sample Calculation of Risk-Based Capital Ratio
for Bank Holding Companies

Example of a banking organization with $6,000 in total capital and the following assets and off-balance sheet items:

Balance Sheet Assets

Cash	$ 5,000
U.S. Treasuries	20,000
Balances at domestic banks	5,000
Loans secured by first liens on 1–4 family residential properties	5,000
Loans to private corporations	65,000
Total balance sheet assets	$100,000

Off-Balance Sheet Items

Standby letters of credit (SLCs) backing general obligation debt issues of U.S. municipalities (GOs)	$ 10,000
Long-term legally binding commitments to private corporations	20,000
Total off-balance sheet items	$ 30,000

This bank holding company's total capital to *total* assets (leverage) ratio would be:

($6,000/$100,000) = 6.00%

To compute the bank holding company's weighted risk assets:

1. Compute the credit equivalent amount of each off-balance sheet (OBS) item.

(*continued*)

TABLE 1 *(continued)*

OBS Item	Face Value		Conversion Factor		Credit Equivalent Amount
SLCs backing municipal GOs	$10,000	×	1.00	=	$10,000
Long-term commitments to private corporations	$20,000	×	0.50	=	$10,000

2. Multiply each balance sheet asset and the credit equivalent amount of each OBS item by the appropriate risk weight.

0% Category

Cash	$ 5,000				
U.S. Treasuries	20,000				
	$25,000	×	0	=	0

20% Category

Balances at domestic banks	$ 5,000				
Credit equivalent amounts of SLCs backing GOs of U.S. municipalities	10,000				
	$15,000	×	0.20	=	$ 3,000

50% Category

Loans secured by first liens on 1–4 family residential properties	$ 5,000	×	0.50	=	$ 2,500

100% Category

Loans to private corporations	$65,000				
Credit equivalent amounts of long-term commitments to private corporations	10,000				
	$75,000	×	1.00	=	$75,000

Total risk-weighted assets	$80,500

This bank holding company's ratio of total capital to weighted risk assets (risk-based capital ratio) would be:

$$(\$6,000/\$80,500) = 7.45\%$$

Source: Board of Governors of the Federal Reserve System.

TABLE 2

Summary Definition of Qualifying Capital for
Bank Holding Companies*
(Using the Year-end 1992 Standards)

Components	Minimum Requirements After Transition Period
Core Capital (Tier 1)	Must equal or exceed 4% of weighted risk assets
Common stockholders' equity	No limit
Qualifying cumulative and noncumulative perpetual preferred stock	Limited to 25% of the sum of common stock, minority interests, and qualifying perpetual preferred stock
Minority interest in equity accounts of consolidated subsidiaries	Organizations should avoid using minority interests to introduce elements not otherwise qualifying for Tier 1 capital
Less: Goodwill[1]	
Supplementary Capital (Tier 2)	Total of Tier 2 is limited to 100% of Tier 1[2]
Allowance for loan and lease losses	Limited to 1.25% of weighted risk assets[2]
Perpetual preferred stock	No limit within Tier 2
Hybrid capital instruments, perpetual debt, and mandatory convertible securities	No limit within Tier 2
Subordinated debt and intermediate-term preferred stock (original weighted average maturity of 5 years or more)	Subordinated debt and intermediate-term preferred stock are limited to 50% of Tier 1;[3] amortized for capital purposes as they approach maturity
Revaluation reserves (equity and building)	Not included: organizations encouraged to disclose; may be evaluated on a case-by-case basis for international comparisons; and taken into account in making an overall assessment of capital.
Deductions (from sum of Tier 1 and Tier 2)	
Investments in unconsolidated subsidiaries	As a general rule, one-half of the aggregate investments will be deducted from Tier 1 capital and one-half from Tier 2 capital.[4]
Reciprocal holdings of banking organizations' capital securities	
Other deductions (such as other subsidiaries or joint ventures) as determined by supervisory authority	On a case-by-case basis or as a matter of policy after formal rulemaking
Total Capital (Tier 1 + Tier 2 − deductions)	Must equal or exceed 8% of weighted risk assets

*See discussion in Section II of the guidelines for a complete description of the requirements for, and the limitations on, the components of qualifying capital.

[1] Goodwill on books of bank holding companies before March 12, 1988, would be "grandfathered" for the transition period.

[2] Amounts in excess of limitations are permitted but do not qualify as capital.

[3] Amounts in excess of limitations are permitted but do not qualify as capital.

[4] A proportionately greater amount may be deducted from Tier 1 capital if the risks associated with the subsidiary so warrant.

173

TABLE 3

Summary of Risk Weights and Risk Categories
for Bank Holding Companies

Category 1: Zero percent

1. Cash (domestic and foreign) held in subsidiary depository institutions or in transit.

2. Balances due from Federal Reserve Banks (including Federal Reserve Bank stock) and central banks in other OECD countries.

3. Direct claims on, and the portions of claims that are unconditionally guaranteed by, the U.S. Treasury and U.S. Government agencies[1], and the central governments of other OECD countries, and local currency claims on, and the portions of local currency claims that are unconditionally guaranteed by, the central governments of non-OECD countries (including the central banks of non-OECD countries), to the extent that subsidiary depository institutions have liabilities booked in that currency.

4. Gold bullion held in the vaults of a subsidiary depository institution or in another's vaults on an allocated basis, to the extent offset by gold bullion liabilities.

Category 2: 20 percent

1. Cash items in the process of collection.

2. All claims (long- or short-term) on, and the portions of claims (long- or short-term) that are guaranteed by, U.S. depository institutions and OECD banks.

3. Short-term claims (remaining maturity of one year or less) on, and the portions of short-term claims that are guaranteed by, non-OECD banks.

4. The portions of claims that are conditionally guaranteed by the central governments of OECD countries and U.S. Government agencies, and the portions of local currency claims that are conditionally guaranteed by the central governments of non-OECD countries, to the extent that subsidiary depository institutions have liabilities booked in that currency.

5. Claims on, and the portions of claims that are guaranteed by, U.S. Government-sponsored agencies.[2]

6. General obligation claims on, and the portions of claims that are guaranteed by the full faith and credit of local governments and political subdivisions of the U.S. and other OECD local governments.

7. Claims on, and the portions of claims that are guaranteed by, official multilateral lending institutions or regional development banks.

8. The portions of claims that are collateralized[3] by securities issued or guaranteed by the U.S. Treasury, the central governments of other OECD countries, U.S. Government agencies, U.S. Government-sponsored agencies, or by cash on deposit in the subsidiary depository institution.

9. The portions of claims that are collateralized[3] by securities issued by official multilateral lending institutions or regional development banks.

10. Certain privately-issued securities representing indirect ownership of mortgage-backed U.S. Government agency or U.S. Government-sponsored agency securities.

11. Investments in shares of a fund whose portfolio is permitted to hold only securities that would qualify for the zero or 20 percent risk categories.

TABLE 3 (*continued*)

Category 3: 50 Percent

1. Loans fully secured by first liens on 1–4 family residential properties that have been made in accordance with prudent underwriting standards, that are performing in accordance with their original terms, and are not past due or in nonaccrual status, and certain privately-issued mortgage-backed securities representing indirect ownership of such loans. (Loans made for speculative purposes are excluded.)

2. Revenue bonds or similar claims that are obligations of U.S. state or local governments, or other OECD local governments, but for which the government entity is committed to repay the debt only out of revenues from the facilities financed.

3. Credit equivalent amounts of interest rate and foreign exchange rate related contracts, except for those assigned to a lower risk category.

Category 4: 100 Percent

1. All other claims on private obligors.

2. Claims on, or guaranteed by, non-OECD foreign banks with a remaining maturity exceeding one year.

3. Claims on, or guaranteed by, non-OECD central governments that are not included in item 3 of Category 1 or item 4 of Category 2; all claims on non-OECD state or local governments.

4. Obligations issued by U.S. state or local governments, or other OECD local governments (including industrial development authorities and similar entities), repayable solely by a private party or enterprise.

5. Premises, plant, and equipment; other fixed assets; and other real estate owned.

6. Investments in any unconsolidated subsidiaries, joint ventures, or associated companies—if not deducted from capital.

7. Instruments issued by other banking organizations that qualify as capital—if not deducted from capital.

8. Claims on commercial firms owned by a government.

9. All other assets, including any intangible assets that are not deducted from capital.

---

[1]For the purpose of calculating the risk-based capital ratio, a U.S. Government agency is defined as an instrumentality of the U.S. Government whose obligations are fully and explicitly guaranteed as to the timely payment of principal and interest by the full faith and credit of the U.S. Government.

[2]For the purpose of calculating the risk-based capital ratio, a U.S. Government-sponsored agency is defined as an agency originally established or chartered to serve public purposes specified by the U.S. Congress but whose obligations are not explicitly guaranteed by the full faith and credit of the U.S. Government.

[3]The extent of collateralization is determined by current market value.

TABLE 4

Credit Conversion Factors for Off-Balance Sheet Items for Bank Holding Companies

100 Percent Conversion Factor

1. Direct credit substitutes. (These include general guarantees of indebtedness and all guarantee-type instruments, including standby letters of credit backing the financial obligations of other parties.)

2. Risk participations in bankers acceptances and direct credit substitutes, such as standby letters of credit.

3. Sale and repurchase agreements and assets sold with recourse that are not included on the balance sheet.

4. Forward agreements to purchase assets, including financing facilities on which drawdown is certain.

5. Securities lent for which the banking organization is at risk.

50 Percent Conversion Factor

1. Transaction-related contingencies. (These include bid bonds, performance bonds, warranties, and standby letters of credit backing the nonfinancial performance of other parties.)

2. Unused portions of commitments with an original maturity[1] exceeding one year, including underwriting commitments and commercial credit lines.

3. Revolving underwriting facilities (RUFs), note issuance facilities (NIFs), and similar arrangements.

20 Percent Conversion Factor

1. Short-term, self-liquidating trade-related contingences, including commercial letters of credit.

Zero Percent Conversion Factor

1. Unused portions of commitments with an original maturity[1] of one year or less, or which are unconditionally cancellable at any time, provided a separate credit decision is made before each drawing.

Credit Conversion for Interest Rate and Foreign Exchange Contracts

The total replacement cost of contracts (obtained by summing the positive mark-to-market values of contracts) is added to a measure of future potential increases in credit exposure. This future potential exposure measure is calculated by multiplying the total notional value of contracts by one of the following credit conversion factors, as appropriate:

Remaining Maturity	*Interest Rate Contracts*	*Exchange Rate Contracts*
One year or less	0	1.0%
Over one year	0.5%	5.0%

No potential exposure is calculated for single currency interest rate swaps in which payments are made based upon two floating rate indices, that is, so called floating/floating or basis swaps. The credit exposure on these contracts is evaluated solely on the basis of their mark-to-market value. Exchange rate contracts with an original maturity of fourteen days or less are excluded. Instruments traded on exchanges that require daily payment of variation margin are also excluded. The only form of netting recognized is netting by novation.

---

[1]Remaining maturity may be used until year-end 1992.

TABLE 5

Calculation of Credit Equivalent Amounts
Interest Rate and Foreign Exchange Rate Related Transactions
for Bank Holding Companies

Type of Contract (remaining maturity)	POTENTIAL EXPOSURE			CURRENT EXPOSURE		CREDIT EQUIVALENT AMOUNT (dollars)
	Notional Principal (dollars) ×	Potential Exposure Conversion Factor =	Potential Exposure (dollars)	+ Replacement Cost[1]	Current Exposure (dollars)[2] =	
1. 120-day forward foreign exchange	5,000,000	.01	50,000	100,000	100,000	150,000
2. 120-day forward foreign exchange	6,000,000	.01	60,000	– 120,000	–0–	60,000
3. 3-year single-currency fixed/floating interest rate swap	10,000,000	.005	50,000	200,000	200,000	250,000
4. 3-year single-currency fixed/floating interest rate swap	10,000,000	.005	50,000	– 250,000	–0–	50,000
5. 7-year cross-currency floating/floating interest rate swap	20,000,000	.05	1,000,000	– 1,300,000	–0–	1,000,000
TOTAL	$51,000,000					$1,510,000

[1]These numbers are purely for illustration.

[2]The larger of zero or a positive mark-to-market value.

177

Index